1

DESIGN FOR A STUDY

OF AMERICAN YOUTH

1

This is the first of a series of reports by the staff of Project TALENT. Subsequent reports will deal with the nature and quality of the American secondary school and with the aptitudes and talents of American youth as revealed by the research described in this volume.

DESIGN FOR A

STUDY OF

AMERICAN YOUTH

John C. Flanagan

John T. Dailey

Marion F. Shaycoft

William A. Gorham

David B. Orr

Isadore Goldberg

HOUGHTON MIFFLIN COMPANY · BOSTON
NEW YORK · ATLANTA · GENEVA, ILL. · DALLAS · PALO ALTO

The research reported herein was performed pursuant to a contract with the United States Office of Education, Department of Health, Education, and Welfare.

BF
431
.F44
1962

HOUGHTON MIFFLIN COMPANY · BOSTON

PRINTED IN THE U.S.A.

CONTENTS

LIST OF TABLES

LIST OF FIGURES

Background of the Study

On April 15, 1959, United States Commissioner of Education Lawrence W. Derthick signed a contract which officially initiated a large-scale, long-range educational research project to determine the best methods for the identification, development, and utilization of human talents. This study was to become known in all parts of the world as Project TALENT.

Upon signing the contract, Commissioner Derthick said: "The purpose of the study is to find out why some students learn and others do not; why some students do poorly in high school and then seem to come into their own in college, while others who do well in high school fail to adjust to college. Here, on an unprecedented scale, is an attempt to find out more about the students' interests, their career plans, and whether the courses they take are consistent with the life objectives they have set for themselves. And above all, it is an attempt to determine why so much of the nation's human potential is lost and what schools, counselors and parents can do to reduce this loss."

Dr. Derthick added: "For many years, educators have been seeking information on these important questions, and while many studies have been conducted in school systems and on a state-wide basis, a study of the magnitude proposed . . . seems to be a highly valuable way to throw . . . light on this subject. . . ."

In approving the contract for Project TALENT, Commissioner Derthick acted under provisions of Public Law 531, passed by Congress in 1954. This unique piece of legislation set up a Cooperative Research Program, authorizing the Commissioner of Education "to enter into contracts or jointly financed cooperative arrangements with universities and colleges . . . for the conduct of research . . . in the field of education."

The Project TALENT contract provided for the allocation of funds to the University of Pittsburgh. Its signing was the culmination of two years of planning by outstanding research workers in the field of education who served as consultants.

Early in 1958, plans for collecting facts regarding the identification, development, and utilization of human talents were already under way at the University of Pittsburgh. These plans attracted the interest and support of a number of government agencies. Among groups providing financial help at that time for the planning phases of the study were the National Science Foundation, National Institute of Mental Health, and the Office of Naval Research. These agencies had expressed interest in the study and wished to share in its support in order to use the findings in planning their own programs. However, as activities under Public Law 531 gathered momentum, these agencies recommended that the research on talent be carried out under the auspices of the Cooperative Research Program, at that time headed by Dr. Roy M. Hall, Assistant Commissioner of Research of the United States Office of Education.

Under law, the Cooperative Research Program is guided by a Research Advisory Committee whose function is to review research proposals submitted to it, and to judge them "as to the soundness of their design, . . . [and] the possibilities of securing productive results. . . ."

In February, 1959, the Research Advisory Committee was headed by Dr. Ralph W. Tyler. Dr. Tyler had been sympathetic from the start toward the main purposes of Project TALENT. But he and his group required, as an official procedure, specific descriptions of the main areas which Project TALENT was to study and the national needs which made such a study necessary. In response to this requirement, the University of Pittsburgh submitted formal proposals for a study designed to collect data from a scientifically selected sample of almost half a million students in secondary schools in all parts of the United States. The facts to be collected from this group of American youth, the proposals stated, were urgently needed to throw more light on seven areas of national concern. Below is the bill of particulars highlighting these seven areas and the reason an inquiry was important in each:

1. *Available talent.*
   More precise information is needed as to the size of the manpower pool qualified for training in science, engineering and other professional fields.

2. *Relations among aptitudes, interests, and other factors.*
   Available knowledge is particularly deficient with respect to the interrelation patterns of aptitudes, preference, interests, socio-economic factors, and motivational factors.

3. *Limiting effects resulting from lack of interest and motivation.*
   Specific information is needed regarding the extent to which people qualified for training in scientific and professional fields lack interest and motivation for obtaining this training.

4. *Factors affecting vocational choice.*
   More information is needed regarding the dynamics of personal decisions and environmental factors which ultimately determine the individual's occupational career pattern.

5. *Predictors of creativity and productivity.*
   Better information is needed with respect to the relation of aptitude, interest, and motivational factors to creativity and productivity in particular professional fields.

6. *Effectiveness of various types of educational experience.*
   Basic information is needed regarding the effectiveness of various types of educational experience in developing special talents.

7. *Procedures for realizing individual potentials.*
   The final overall requirement is for sound information regarding procedures for assisting the individual to realize his highest potential.

After reviewing the proposals for Project TALENT, Dr. Tyler and his Research Advisory Committee met in Washington for a three-day session (February 12 to 14, 1959) to discuss them along with proposals for other research studies. It was at this meeting that the Committee recommended to the Commissioner of Education that Project TALENT was worthy of support by the United States Office of Education.

2

Project TALENT was designed to help provide answers to what Commissioner Derthick described in 1959 as "one of the most crucial problems in education." However, the origins of the project go back to another critical time in the history of the nation — World War II. In 1941, when this country was mobilizing its manpower resources and was faced with the problem of identifying the young men who could be trained to fill many wartime duty assignments, a young psychologist, Dr. John C. Flanagan, was commissioned as a major in the Army Air Forces to direct the classification activities of the Aviation Psychology Program.

His first and most urgent assignment was to devise procedures for identifying and training the tens of thousands of cadets required to man the planes needed to meet the challenge of the Nazi and Japanese air forces. To meet these demands, the traditional educational requirements for aviation cadet training were eliminated; new selection and classification procedures based on aptitudes for each type of job were developed.

Under the new procedures, young men who qualified on the first mental and physical screening tests given by the Aviation Cadet Boards were sent to Aircrew Classification Centers. Here they were given a battery of aptitude classification tests which required a day and a half to complete. In addition to serving as a classification instrument, this battery of 20 tests also became the subject of continuous study, evaluation, and refinement throughout the war.

In 1943 Lt. Colonel Flanagan and his Air Force psychologists decided to see how well the 20 tests predicted the future performance of young men in intensive emergency pilot training. One thousand applicants who had passed the first physical screening tests were accepted and sent into pilot training regardless of their qualifications as indicated on the aptitude classification tests.

The value of the tests was dramatically demonstrated when only sixteen out of the 442 men who had the lowest pilot aptitude scores successfully completed pilot training. By contrast, nearly all those with the highest pilot aptitude scores successfully completed the pilot training courses.

The predictive value of these tests saved hundreds of millions of dollars in training costs and greatly increased the quality of performance of pilots sent into combat. Of even greater long-range significance was the large-scale demonstration of the practical importance of various patterns of aptitudes.

The results in the Aviation Psychology Program in World War II clearly indicated that the aptitudes important for success in one job were often quite different from those in another job. Individuals who failed to solo in primary pilot training because of extreme ineptness frequently were later graduated at the top of their class in navigation training.

After returning to civilian life, the Air Force psychologists began to study civilian jobs in terms of aptitudes and abilities required for success. They identified the requirements for different types of jobs, and developed tests to predict effective performance in the tasks important for these jobs.

But there are hundreds of different kinds of jobs in the civilian labor market; and follow-up studies in civilian life are expensive and time-consuming. So, even though in the 1950's public demands for better guidance programs for students began to increase, the data required to match talents and tasks with a high degree of confidence were not available.

In 1957 the United States was jolted by the challenge of totalitarian technological advances. And at the same time, our country found itself possessing new tools for developing our human resources. Scientific breakthroughs in electronic data processing made it feasible to do long-range studies on large populations. Newly-developed tests appeared to provide measures for all the important job elements that had been identified in post-war studies of critical job requirements. Above all, public opinion recognized the increasing national need for scientific methods in improving education, creativity, and productivity. Leaders in government and education recognized, too, the need for new information, without which orderly progress in developing human resources would be impossible.

3

In 1957, Colonel John C. Flanagan, now professor of psychology at the University of Pittsburgh and president of the American Institute for Research, developed a proposal for a study of sufficient scope to provide the United States with the kinds of information critically needed by education, industry, government, and the military services. As noted earlier, this proposal was submitted to a number of foundations and government agencies. After a series of conferences, the National Science Foundation, the National Institute of Mental Health, the Office of Naval Research, and the Cooperative Research Program of the United States Office of Education agreed in October, 1957, to support a planning study to investigate the feasibility of the project and to develop detailed procedures for carrying it out. Two years of review and planning followed.

After consulting with many individuals and groups, four advisory panels were established in March, 1958. The panel members were selected to be as competent and representative as possible. The original chairman of the combined groups was Dr. John H. Fischer, then Superintendent of the Baltimore Public Schools. When Dr. Fischer became dean of Teachers College, Columbia University, the chairmanship was assumed by Dr. Kenneth E. Oberholtzer, Superintendent of the Denver Public Schools. The list of advisory panels and the members of each is as follows:

ADVISORY PANELS

Guidance and Counseling Panel

Chairman (Initial), Dr. Donald E. Super, Professor of Education, Department of Psychological Foundations and Services, Teachers College, Columbia University

** Chairman, Edward Landy, Director, Division of Counseling Services, Newton (Massachusetts) Public Schools

Ralph F. Berdie, Director, Student Counseling Bureau, University of Minnesota

Bruce E. Shear, Chief, Bureau of Guidance, New York State Education Department

John M. Stalnaker, President, National Merit Scholarship Corporation

David V. Tiedeman, Associate Professor of Education, Harvard University

Arthur E. Traxler, Executive Director, Educational Records Bureau

Leona E. Tyler, Professor of Psychology, University of Oregon

Testing Problems Panel

Chairman, Robert L. Thorndike, Head, Department of Psychological Foundations and Services, Teachers College, Columbia University

Henry Chauncey, President, Educational Testing Service

Wayne H. Holtzman, Associate Director, Hogg Foundation, University of Texas

A. Paul Horst, Professor of Psychology, University of Washington

Lloyd G. Humphreys, Chairman, Department of Psychology, University of Illinois

E. Lowell Kelly, Director, Bureau of Psychological Services, University of Michigan

Joseph Zubin, Principal Research Scientist, Biometrics Research Unit, New York State Department of Mental Hygiene

Educational Research Panel

Chairman, Robert J. Keller, Director, University High School, University of Minnesota

Frank D. Ashburn, Headmaster, Brooks School (Massachusetts)

** Paul L. Banfield, Headmaster, Landon School (Maryland)

Reverend O'Neil C. D'Amour, Assistant to the Executive Secretary, National Catholic Education Association

Warren G. Findley, Assistant Superintendent for Pupil Personnel Services, Atlanta Public Schools

Earl J. McGrath, Professor of Education, Teachers College, Columbia University

Paul T. Rankin, Assistant Superintendent of Schools, Detroit Public Schools

James W. Reynolds, Professor of Education, University of Texas

J. Wayne Wrightstone, Director, Bureau of Educational Research, New York City Board of Education

Manpower and Sociology Panel

* Chairman, Samuel A. Stouffer, Director, Laboratory of Social Relations, Harvard University

E. Franklin Frazier, Head, Department of Sociology, Howard University

Seymour E. Harris, Chairman, Department of Economics, Harvard University

* Irving D. Lorge, Executive Officer, Institute of Psychological Research, Teachers College, Columbia University

Donald G. Marquis, Massachusetts Institute of Technology

C. Joseph Nuesse, Dean, School of Social Science, Catholic University of America

Fred L. Strodtbeck, Associate Professor of Sociology, University of Chicago

* Deceased
** Replacement

During the first year, Dr. Robert C. Craig was the only full-time member of the staff. In June, 1958, Dr. John T. Dailey replaced Dr. Craig as the full-time director of the project. Other staff members who worked with Dr. Dailey included Miss Marion F. Shaycoft, and Drs. William A. Gorham, David B. Orr, and Isadore Goldberg. The staff worked closely with the advisory panels who met in Washington for a series of two-day planning sessions.

By December, 1958, the various advisory panels had made their final recommendations, the planning study was completed, and the revised proposal was submitted to the Cooperative Research Program of the United States Office of Education. The Research Advisory Committee of that Program recommended that the study be given support. Commissioner Derthick reviewed the recommendations, concurred in the advice of the Committee, and in April, 1959, signed the contract for Project TALENT. The staff of the U.S. Office of Education continued its support and assistance to the project under Commissioner Sterling M. McMurrin.

Work began immediately. The advisory panels had recommended using a two-day battery of tests specifically developed for this project. The staff had already begun work on the materials. After these materials were reviewed by the panels, the experimental forms of the tests were tried out in May, 1959, in eleven high schools in five states.

It was agreed that the final forms of the tests would be given to nearly half a million students in secondary schools throughout the country. The task of simultaneously testing so large a number in widely separated parts of the country posed great administrative problems. Once the scientifically stratified random sample of schools had been selected it became necessary to enlist the help of school superintendents, principals, and teachers all over the United States. On the basis of the geographic locations of the various schools selected for the sample, 90 regional coordinators were appointed to work with the educational personnel at state, city, and school levels who were responsible for the secondary schools that had been selected for participation in Project TALENT. These regional coordinators assumed responsibility for coordinating and assisting in administering the two-day test battery. They also collected data about these schools, their curricula, staff, guidance programs, and future plans. The regional coordinators for Project TALENT included:

REGIONAL COORDINATORS

Alabama
> Paul R. Givens, Birmingham-Southern College
> Herbert Eber, Birmingham

Arizona
> Richard E. Schutz, Arizona State University, Tempe

Arkansas
> Carter Short, University of Arkansas, Fayetteville
> Hardy C. Wilcoxon, University of Arkansas, Fayetteville

California
> Alex D. Aloia, Loyola University of Los Angeles
> John Caffrey, Director of Research, Palo Alto Unified School District
> Frederick J. McDonald, Stanford University, Palo Alto

Colorado
> Anthony C. Tucker, University of Denver

Connecticut
> Joseph Raymond Gerberich, University of Connecticut, Storrs

Delaware
> Arthur R. DeLong, University of Delaware, Newark

District of Columbia
> William A. Gorham, University of Pittsburgh

Florida
> Edward Caldwell, Board of Public Instruction, Manatee County, Bradenton
> John V. McQuitty, University of Florida, Gainesville

Georgia
  Cameron Fincher, Georgia State College for Business Administration, Atlanta
  G. H. Fort, Board of Education, Atlanta
  Richard H. Kicklighter, Gainesville, Florida
  R. T. Osborne, University of Georgia, Athens

Idaho
  Elwyn DeLaurier, State Guidance Supervisor, Department of Education, Boise

Illinois
  N. L. Gage, University of Illinois, Champaign
  Lyman J. Smith, Illinois State Scholarship Commission, Deerfield

Indiana
  N. A. Fattu, University of Indiana, Bloomington
  H. H. Remmers, Purdue University, Lafayette

Iowa
  Arthur Mittman, University of Iowa, Iowa City
  Gordon J. Rhum, Iowa State Teachers College, Cedar Falls
  Herbert M. Silvey, Iowa State Teachers College, Cedar Falls

Kansas
  Kenneth E. Anderson, University of Kansas, Lawrence
  Charles B. Watkins, Guidance and Personnel Service, Kansas State Department of Public Instruction, Topeka

Kentucky
  Ernest McDaniel, University of Kentucky, Lexington

Louisiana
  Robert N. Vidulich, Louisiana State University, Baton Rouge

Maine
  David R. Fink, Jr., University of Maine, Orono

Maryland
  Robert C. Lloyd, Baltimore Public Schools

Massachusetts
  Seth Arsenian, Springfield College
  George S. Elias, Springfield College
  Edward Scanlon, Division of Counseling Services, Newton Public Schools, West Newton

Michigan
  Claude L. Nemzek, University of Detroit
  * Edwin G. Spacie, Central Michigan University, Mt. Pleasant
  Buford Stefflre, Michigan State University, East Lansing
  Frank B. Womer, University of Michigan, Ann Arbor

Minnesota
  Ralph F. Berdie, Director, Student Counseling Bureau, University of Minnesota
  Robert J. Keller, Director, University High School, University of Minnesota
Mississippi
  Roscoe A. Boyer, University of Mississippi, University
  Russell W. Levanway, Millsaps College, Jackson
Missouri
  Joseph L. French, University of Missouri, Columbia
  Robert E. Lefton, Psychological Associates, Clayton
Montana
  William A. Garrison, Eastern Montana College of Education, Billings
Nebraska
  Warren Baller, University of Nebraska, Lincoln
New Hampshire
  Paul McIntire, University of New Hampshire, Durham
New Jersey
  Albert S. Thompson, Teachers College, Columbia University, New York
New Mexico
  Virginia Keehan, Department of Education, Santa Fe
New York
  Warren W. Coxe, Delmar
  S. David Farr, University of Buffalo
  Harold Howes, Milne High School, Albany
  John M. Skalski, Fordham University, New York
  * Percival M. Symonds, Professor Emeritus, Teachers College, Columbia University, New York
  Clarence M. Williams, University of Rochester
North Carolina
  Roy N. Anderson, North Carolina State College, Raleigh
  Junius A. Davis, University of North Carolina, Greensboro
  Thomas E. Jeffrey, University of North Carolina, Chapel Hill
  William D. Perry, University of North Carolina, Chapel Hill
North Dakota
  Ralph H. Kolstoe, University of North Dakota, Grand Forks
  Robert E. Larson, State Agricultural College, Fargo
  Grant M. Norem, State Teachers College, Minot
Ohio
  Howard B. Lyman, University of Cincinnati
  Walter S. Nosal, John Carroll University, Cleveland
  Ray Wood, Columbus

Oklahoma
W. R. Brown, University of Oklahoma, Norman
Oregon
J. Spencer Carlson, University of Oregon, Eugene
Pennsylvania
L. Kathryn Dice, Department of Public Instruction, Harrisburg
Roy B. Hackman, Temple University, Philadelphia
C. Mauritz Lindvall, University of Pittsburgh
Rhode Island
Frances E. Dunn, Brown University, Providence
South Carolina
R. L. Kalmbach, Columbia Public Schools, Columbia
W. C. McCall, University of South Carolina, Columbia
Donna S. Young, University of South Carolina, Columbia
South Dakota
V. Gregory Rosemont, Huron College, Huron
Tennessee
George E. Copple, Vanderbilt University, Nashville
Louise W. Cureton, Knoxville
Texas
Robert P. Anderson, Texas Technological College, Lubbock
H. Paul Kelley, University of Texas, Austin
Saul B. Sells, Texas Christian University, Fort Worth
Franklin L. Stovall, University of Houston
David F. Votaw, Sr., San Marcos
Utah
Hyrum M. Smith, Department of Public Instruction, Salt Lake
City
Virginia
Richard L. Beard, University of Virginia, Charlottesville
Donald J. Herrmann, College of William and Mary, Williams-
burg
Washington
William C. Budd, Western Washington College of Education,
Bellingham
Glen E. Maier, Eastern Washington College of Education,
Cheney
West Virginia
Walter Jarecke, University of West Virginia, Morgantown
Wisconsin
Elden A. Bond, Milwaukee Public Schools
Robert C. Craig, Marquette University, Milwaukee
Ralph H. Tindall, Milwaukee Public Schools, Milwaukee

Wyoming
  R. Duane Andrews, Department of Education, Cheyenne
  * Deceased

The thinking and planning of the Project TALENT staff were also guided by an Advisory Council. The Council held two meetings, the first in November of 1959, the second in November of 1960. Following are the names of those who attended one or both of these meetings:

  Dugald S. Arbuckle, President, American Personnel and Guidance Association
  Brother Bartholomew, CFX, President, Secondary School Dept., National Catholic Education Association
  Charles F. Carroll, President, Council of Chief State School Officers
  The Rt. Rev. Msgr. O'Neil D'Amour, Associate Secretary of the School Superintendent's Department, National Catholic Education Association
  Roy O. Frantz, President, National School Boards Association
  Edgar Fuller, Executive Secretary, Council of Chief State School Officers
  Arthur A. Hitchcock, Executive Secretary, American Personnel and Guidance Association
  Paul E. Klopsteg, President, American Association for the Advancement of Science
  Chauncey D. Leake, President, American Association for the Advancement of Science
  Kenneth E. Oberholtzer, Superintendent, Denver Public Schools
  W. A. Shannon, Executive Director, National School Boards Association
  George E. Watson, President, Council of Chief State School Officers
  Dael Wolfle, Administrative Secretary, American Association for the Advancement of Science

4

The year 1960 was a census year. The United States government was taking inventory of the number of persons who made up the population of the country. This census provided statistics on the total number of people and their major characteristics. It seemed propitious that 1960 also was the year for Project TALENT to launch the first national census of the aptitudes and abilities of the young people in the secondary schools of the country.

To provide professional advice on the selection of a representative sample of schools and institutions, the staff enlisted the aid of a committee of sampling experts. This group consisted of Morris H. Hansen, Assistant Director for Research and Development, Bureau of the Census; William G. Cochran, Professor of Statistics, Harvard University; Phillip J. Rulon, Professor of Education, Harvard University; and Frederick F. Stephan, Professor of Social Statistics, Princeton University.

By January of 1960 all the tests had been prepared and tried out. Ninety-three per cent of the schools selected had indicated their willingness to participate in the project and the administrative arrangements for testing had been made with the schools.

In March of 1960, some 440,000 students in 1,353 public, private, and parochial secondary schools in all parts of the country took the Project TALENT tests. The work of the regional coordinators in cooperation with state, city, and local school officials, and with teachers had been a success. The first data collection phase of Project TALENT was completed when the classroom teachers, in cooperation with school guidance counselors, administered the tests to the students, collected the answer sheets, and returned them to the Project TALENT test scoring headquarters at the Measurement Research Center at the State University of Iowa. There Dr. E. F. Lindquist directed the massive job of scoring, recording, and reporting the more than one billion bits of information collected from the students. Rosters of scores made on all tests by the students who participated in the project were sent to their individual schools.

At the same time, the staff of Project TALENT began to analyze the data — an undertaking which will provide the information to help America reassess its educational program and its human resources.

ACKNOWLEDGMENTS

Writing this volume has been a cooperative venture on the part of the entire Project TALENT staff. However, the following individuals prepared the original drafts of the various chapters:

The Overview and Chapters 1 and 2 — Dr. John C. Flanagan, Responsible Investigator for this study; Chapter 3 — Dr. John T. Dailey, Program Director, and Marion F. Shaycoft, Supervisor for Measurement Studies; Chapter 4 — Miss Shaycoft; Chapter 5 — Miss Shaycoft and Dr. Dailey; Chapter 6 — Miss Shaycoft and Dr. Dailey; Chapter 7 — Dr. David B. Orr, Supervisor for School Characteristics Studies; Chapters 8 and 9 — Dr. Isadore Goldberg, Supervisor for Manpower and Guidance Studies; Chapter 10 — Dr. William A. Gorham, Supervisor for Special Studies; Chapter 11 — Miss Shaycoft and Dr. Dailey; Chapter 12 — Dr. Orr; Chapter 13 — Dr. Goldberg; Chapter 14 — Dr. Orr.

Under the over-all direction of Dr. Flanagan and Dr. Dailey, primary responsibility for various aspects of the developmental phases covered in this volume was allocated as follows:

Marion S. Shaycoft, Aptitude and Achievement Test Editor; William A. Gorham, Supervisor of Test Administration; David B. Orr, Student Activities Inventory and School Data Form Editor; Isadore Goldberg, Interest and Student Information Blank Editor.

The following individuals reviewed some of the experimental forms of the tests: John B. Carroll, Paul Diederich, Paul Dressel, Max Engelhart, Grace Fivars, Geraldine Spaulding, Machlin Thomas, and Mary Willis. Grace Fivars wrote the first drafts of the Creativity test; Mary Willis wrote the first draft of the Mechanical Reasoning test; and Geraldine Spaulding reviewed the final forms of all the tests. Joyce Brueckel, Bertha Harper, and Nathan Jaspen advised on planning the analysis.

Clinton A. Neyman, Jr., Supervisor for Services, assisted in many of the production and technical aspects of the project.

Finally, the staff wishes to acknowledge the help of Ben Brodinsky, Editor-in-Chief, Croft Educational Services, New London, Conn., for his editorial guidance in preparing this report.

Much of the technical data in this volume was based on the Project TALENT Monograph Series, Monograph No. 1, "Designing the Study," December, 1960. Copies of this monograph were filed with the United States Office of Education, pursuant to the contract with the Cooperative Research Program, United States Office of Education, Department of Health, Education, and Welfare.

1 The Importance
of Understanding Talent

Our nation pays a high price for its inadequate understanding of talent. Therefore, we begin by exploring the background and issues of three questions: What is talent? How can it be developed? How can the individual make the best use of his talents?

We discover that talent does not consist of intelligence alone. We recount the famous war-time experiment of the Air Force in which a new concept of talent contributed to victory. We outline the need for a more widespread application of the lessons of the Air Force experience.

Finally, we examine briefly a most important agency in the United States for the development of talent — the secondary school; and we meet Robert, one of a half million young persons, whose pattern of aptitudes and abilities will either be developed or neglected in the years ahead. We state that the purpose of our study is to see how Robert's talents (and those of all American youth in the future) can be brought to a point of high productivity and usefulness.

The physical scientist who explores molecular patterns with a beam of X-rays and the behavioral scientist who explores a student's intellectual patterns with a series of objective test items are engaged in tasks of similar challenge. The physical scientist probes the mysteries of the molecule. The behavioral scientist seeks to pierce the riddle of man's intellect. Both face cosmic enigmas and work under an identical urgency to gain understanding of the forces of nature.

The pattern of the beam of X-rays as diffracted by the molecules of a crystal is indistinct. The physical scientist must do considerable estimating — checking and rechecking his computations with high-speed electronic computers — before he can draw a model of a complex molecule.

A student's pattern of answers to test questions is usually even more difficult to interpret, and many samples are required before the profile of the student's capacities and limitations can be even tentatively estimated.

Difficult though the task of interpreting the many samples of a student's talents may be, each young person needs a clear picture of himself if he is to develop his highest potentials. A nation, too, needs a clear picture of the total talents and abilities of its people. Such a picture can come only from the scientific study of man. Such study is now possible. Our tools and methods for the scientific study of man are still crude, crude as the ancient Chinese abacus, yet there is no reason to abandon or condemn them. Without the abacus, high-speed electronic computers could not have been developed.

Limited as our methods for the study of people are, they are beginning to yield important and useful concepts for the improvement of our behavior, our institutions, and our modes of thinking. Equally important is the fact that we now know the directions in which our investigations of people should move. We know the avenues to explore.

One of the most important of these tasks is charting the complex intellectual patterns which determine those fields in which a man can perform, achieve, and create.

This is the task with which we in Project TALENT have concerned ourselves during the past two years. It is a task we shall continue to pursue for the next decade and longer. But even now some promising results are beginning to emerge. To understand these, as well as the research findings that will become available over the next several years, it will be necessary to understand the conditions which led to the plans we developed and the questions we hope to answer.

One important factor is that our lack of definitive knowledge of the capabilities of men is a serious handicap to the nation — its industries, armed forces, professions, and arts and sciences.

The employer who assigns a $10,000-a-year engineer to draft the design specifications that a $7,000-a-year draftsman could do better and with greater satisfaction to all involved is wasting money and talent.

The college admissions officer who looks only at a high school graduate's grades and scholastic test scores is seeing just part of the student. How many young people with outstanding specific aptitudes are being overlooked by colleges and universities because of our inadequate measures of potential ability?

The guidance counselor who has no tools for predicting whether Johnny will have greater success in accounting or in mechanics falls short of performing a service much needed by Johnny, industry, and the nation.

The civil service official who insists that only "persons of high intelligence" can qualify for jobs in which clerical ability is more important than broad mental powers is wasting the taxpayers' money and vitally needed manpower resources.

We could give hundreds of examples of waste, misuse, and abuse of human ability. Taken together, the national waste of human resources is appalling. Anyone assigning a dollar value to the squander of human talents will be wide of the mark — and there is no way to begin to estimate the additional cost in frustration and unhappiness for the individuals whose time and effort go into activities which bring them little satisfaction.

Can these losses be turned into gains? Searching for ways and techniques to accomplish this is one of the purposes of Project TALENT. We are not alone in this search. Much has already been done, and much related work is continuing in the United States and in other parts of the world. The efficient application of the talents of each man, woman, and child is the concern of governments as well as parents, teachers, psychologists, personnel directors, and military officers.

There are three fundamental questions we must answer: What is talent? How can it be developed? How can an individual make the best use of his talents?

2

What is talent?

The definition of talent in a primitive tribe is likely to be quite simple. Where the tribe depends primarily on hunting wild game for survival, the definition of talent will focus on the ability to become an outstanding hunter. To the warring tribe, the ability to carry battle to the enemy is most prized.

Even nations which produced men whose brilliant insights and ideas are still recognized today had a limited view of man's talents. The Greeks honored the orator and the artist — but failed to appreciate the inventor. Rome cherished the soldier and the administrator — but failed to recognize the many other potential talents of either its citizens or its slaves.

What is our present concept of talent and how has it developed? It is not surprising that a complex society such as ours has a complex view of talents. But events of the recent past strongly emphasize that the systematic study of talent is still in its infancy. Some progress has been made in gaining the understanding essential to the development of a science of human behavior. However, let us review its most recent stage of development. Even now the effects of the period of oversimplification of the concept of talent linger in many places.

This oversimplified concept of the basis of talent was the theory of general intelligence. This theory might be regarded as representing a stage of development roughly analogous to that of the early theory of phlogiston in the physical sciences. Although the phlogiston theory has been abandoned, it was a milestone of man's progress from alchemy to our present concepts of physical science.

The phlogiston theory was developed by two German chemists, Johann J. Becher and Georg E. Stahl, in the latter part of the seventeenth century. It was Stahl who formalized and named its components. The phlogiston theory stated that metals were composed of a *calx*, different for each metal, and *phlogiston* which was the material of fire and which was consumed when a combustible substance burned. This theory was widely accepted for nearly a century because it appeared to provide a neat explanation for many of the observed characteristics of combustion. The careful quantitative studies of the English scientist, Henry Cavendish, revealed many weaknesses in the phlogiston theory; but even Cavendish never quite discarded the theory entirely. Late in the eighteenth century, the French chemist, Antoine L. Lavoisier, described the nature of chemical elements essentially as they are known today and is generally credited with having replaced the out-moded phlogiston theory with a more useful one.

Let us trace the parallel development and replacement of the theory of general intelligence. Early in the 1900's Alfred Binet, the French psychologist, began working on a set of practical tests of intellect. Binet studied examples in which the higher mental processes were exhibited in handling simple, practical problems.

Following the work of the great English social scientist, Francis Galton, Binet worked toward establishing individual psychology on a scientific basis by trying out his tests on writers, artists, mathematicians, and chess players, as well as school children. The scales for the measurement of intelligence and educational attainment which he developed and prepared for the school children of Paris were copied all over the world. They have been widely used in the measurement of intelligence in this country in the series of revised forms prepared by Lewis M. Terman and his associates, and known as the Stanford-Binet tests of intelligence. Binet's tests had a profound effect throughout the world because they provided a series of tasks standardized according to the average age at which they could be successfully performed by most children. In this way, a scale of mental ages was provided which later led to a method for obtaining the ratio of mental to chronological age, known as the Intelligence Quotient or I.Q. This convenient ratio, which conveys essentially the same meaning regardless of a child's chronological age, provided a useful index which was universally adopted as the standard procedure for describing the level of a child's intellectual potential. Binet's original scale was intended only as a practical, useful test, and he did not draw theoretical implications from his findings.

The theoretical case for general intelligence came from the work of Charles Spearman, who retired from an active military career in the British army to study the new field of psychology in Germany. He received his Ph.D. degree at the age of 40. When Spearman returned to England he joined a group at Oxford University who were using Karl Pearson's recently developed mathematical index — the correlation coefficient — for studying the relations between various test scores and other measures of ability. The group at Oxford was formed to develop tests of intelligence to be used in a projected survey of British schools planned by Francis Galton.

Spearman's work on this project led him to publish a paper in 1904 entitled, "General Intelligence: Objectively Determined and Measured." At about this same time, Binet was publishing his Intelligence Scales for use with the school children of Paris. Spearman studied the correlations between the scores on a wide variety of tests, school grades, and teachers' ratings and concluded that all such performance was dependent on the amount of general intelligence which the individual possessed, plus a second factor which was different for each type of content (verbal, numerical, etc.). Thus, all forms of human behavior were to be explained by (1) a factor specific to the content, paralleling the calx of each metal in the phlogiston theory, and (2) general intelligence, called "g." Spearman's "g" was, in effect, the common element in human performance, analogous to the phlogiston supposedly common to all metals.

These notions, gradually discarded, had at least one beneficial outcome. American researchers of individual differences, including Karl J. Holzinger, Truman Lee Kelley, L. L. Thurstone and J. P. Guilford, were attracted by the objective measures and precise statistical analyses that were an important part of the "g" theory. They were stimulated to study the dimensions of intellect.

Strong support for Spearman's theory came from a new source — the success of the Binet Scales and the Army Alpha Group Tests of Intelligence used to classify men in World War I. Following World War I, Arthur S. Otis and others published group tests of general intelligence which made it convenient and inexpensive to obtain estimates of the I.Q.'s of large numbers of students. These developments established general intelligence and the I.Q. as the sole and exclusive indicators of aptitude and intellectual ability, at least in the popular mind. However, a few psychologists, notably Truman Lee Kelley at Harvard, and L. L. Thurstone at the University of Chicago, had doubts that "g," or general intelligence, the phlogiston of Spearman's theory, was indeed the universal factor that Spearman presumed it to be.

Through the work of Kelley and Thurstone, several mental factors were established. These included: memory, reasoning, ability to do simple arithmetic, to understand word meanings, to note small changes in visual details, and to identify objects which had been rotated.

In spite of these promising research studies, general intelligence was still the basis for nearly all practical testing of intellect in 1941, when a group of younger psychologists were invited into the military service to assist in selecting and classifying young men for training as aviation cadets. The psychologists directing this work had been students of Kelley and Thurstone and they immediately began planning, developing, applying, and testing the multifactor theories in an effort to help the Army Air Forces with the task of defending America.

3

To meet the blows of Hitler's Luftwaffe, the U. S. Army Air Forces had to recruit hurriedly, train, and send into combat large numbers of aircrews. Pilot, navigator, bombardier — these three constituted a flying team, and on their skill depended much of America's security from 1941 to 1945. The pilot was the leader of the three; young men vied for the honor and challenge of the pilot's job. Applicants for flight training were selected on traditional criteria at that time — the number of years spent in school or college, and scores on general intelligence or screening tests. Those who failed in pilot training were considered for training as navigators or bombardiers.

This was wasteful and inefficient; it ignored the nature of the various tasks which members of an aircrew had to perform. That was the argument used by the group of psychologists who were working on the selection problem for the Army Air Forces. The theories they tested in a series of studies were later reported in the Research Reports of the Army Air Force Aviation Psychology Program. These studies first demonstrated the feasibility of large-scale programs of the type proposed for Project TALENT.

First the psychologists took a long, hard look at the types of tasks which each man in an aircrew had to perform. They determined that the tasks were distinctive — they differed for each of the three jobs, and they required distinctive aptitudes. For example, the pilot required a high degree of understanding of mechanical principles in order to be able to visualize the responses of planes to controls and special conditions; the navigator needed special aptitude for interpreting charts, maps, and gauges; the bombardier needed to be skillful in identifying specific patterns and objects (enemy gun installations or munitions factories) from high altitudes.

The Air Force psychologists established the fact that a different pattern of job elements was critical to the success of each of the three types of aircrew jobs. They tackled the problem of identifying these particular patterns of aptitudes in the thousands of applicants who were eager to enter flight training — to find the men best suited for each of these three vital assignments.

In answer to this need, they developed the Aircrew Classification Tests — tests to measure each of the aptitudes required for effective performance in the three aircrew jobs. This battery of twenty aptitude and ability tests was administered to hundreds of thousands of young men before the war ended in 1945.

The Air Force psychologists worked on the theory that young men who scored high in tests of pilot aptitude could successfully complete pilot training; that those whose scores for pilot aptitude were low should not be sent into training since they could not be expected to complete the training successfully. The psychologists felt equally certain that the men whose scores for navigator aptitude or for bombardier aptitude were high were likely to succeed as navigators and bombardiers.

Was this a sound theory? Follow-up studies of thousands of men selected on the basis of their aptitude scores on the Aircrew Classification Tests demonstrated clearly that the psychologists' predictions based on the scores made by those who applied for training were good predictions. The practical value of the Aircrew Classification Tests to the selection and classification program of the Air Forces and the war effort was obvious. Through these tests it was possible to provide the air training schools with a continuous flow of cadets who could successfully complete their training courses as pilots, navigators, and bombardiers and take their places as members of the air crews in America's flying fortresses.

By the end of the war it was evident that psychological testing had paid off. The Air Force had saved millions of dollars in equipment and training time, and hundreds of thousands of young men were assigned to wartime jobs in which they could serve their country best.

The wartime experiences in testing added to our store of knowledge of human talents. We now had a new dimension of individual differences — we knew that each person possesses his own unique pattern of aptitudes. The fact that one pattern of aptitudes made one man a good pilot while quite a different pattern of aptitudes made his friend a good navigator was an important finding. Of even greater importance was the discovery that these individual and trait differences in aptitudes persist over long periods of time. Intensive training periods and new training methods did little to help the person to succeed if his aptitudes did not fit the pattern required by the job.

These facts caused us to abandon the phlogiston-type concept of general intelligence and move on to the new concepts tested during World War II.

What are these new concepts of human ability? What is the current view of behavioral scientists regarding the nature of talents? There have been many efforts to relate observed patterns of intellectual performance to electrical activity in the brain as measured by the electro-encephalograph; to differences in speed of conduction of an individual's nerves; to variations in his body chemistry; and to head size or body proportions. None of these efforts has developed a promising relationship with observed individual differences. Therefore, in measuring an individual's talents at the present time we must rely entirely on his performance of sample tasks. Most of these sample tasks will not be new to the individual. Furthermore, in addition to his natural talent for a task, the individual's performance will reflect the extent of his training and previous experience with this task, thus complicating our interpretation of his talents. Although the problem of measuring human talents is, therefore, difficult and complicated at the present time, and the measurements cannot be regarded as precise, they can be useful in assisting the individual in identifying the nature of his unique pattern of talents.

Under present circumstances an individual's talent must be defined as his unique pattern of potentials for learning to perform various types of activities important in our culture. Such a definition includes potential to learn to perform on a musical instrument, to paint, or to act. But our definition also includes potential to learn the more common activities such as preparing food, repairing electrical and mechanical devices, cabinet making, designing, telling stories, taking part in athletic sports, teaching, and administering and managing.

Present evidence suggests that individuals whose performance is high with respect to one aptitude also tend to excel in others. However, there are many notable exceptions of individuals having outstanding talent (potential to learn) in one field and below average potential in most other fields. To repeat, talent represents only potential ability to learn and must be developed. There are an infinite number of patterns and combinations of talents present in our young people, and it is important that each individual be assisted in identifying his unique pattern of talents.

What do we mean by a pattern of aptitudes and abilities? For John, Mary, or Willis, such a pattern might consist in part of (1) high ability to understand typical paragraphs of reading material; (2) poor performance on the various tests of English expression, such as punctuation, capitalization, English usage; (3) slowness in checking clerical materials and in arithmetic computation; (4) relatively good performance on arithmetic reasoning, but only average ability to handle typical secondary school mathematics problems; (5) little insight into mechanical relations, and (6) poor ability to visualize movements in two or three dimensions.

We might place beside such indicators of talent other factors from personal and family background: (1) a home in which there are many books; (2) a father who completed only one year of college, who earns a relatively high wage; (3) a family with high aspiration for their sons, but with the straightforward goal of early marriage for their daughters.

How many of the groups of students having this pattern of ability (or any one of a thousand different combinations) will go to college, and in what occupations will they be successful? What personal factors, such as parental influence or early marriage, will help or hinder these young people in developing their talents and using them most effectively?

To some extent, we can now identify the combination of aptitudes and abilities which are necessary to do well in a liberal arts college course. Similarly, the combination required for success in an engineering course has been fairly well established. However, for many important occupations the requirements for success have been only vaguely outlined.

The Air Force research, and the concepts that grew out of it, showed that we could identify and put to use with precision the talents needed for three wartime tasks of crucial importance. Now we need to identify a vastly broader range of talents crucial to the peacetime economy and to national technological and cultural progress.

To achieve this, it is necessary to have an adequate setting for carrying on research — a setting in which large numbers of people can be observed for long periods of time. Anything less will not do — as one postwar experience has already proved. Shortly after demobilization, the Air Force psychologists attempted to develop aptitude classification test batteries for peacetime jobs. The tests were given to high school students. These students were then followed up after they had entered college or had gone into various occupations. But the results were not conclusive. The numbers were small as compared with the hundreds of thousands of cadets whose records were readily available and who were relatively easy to follow into their careers as pilots, navigators, and bombardiers. By contrast, the widely scattered high school students in the peacetime studies moved from city to city, entered many different colleges and universities, and many hundreds of different occupations. The number of young people entering any one career was too small to provide the basis for good predictions of what makes for success or failure in that particular occupation.

Consequently, fifteen years after the war very few of the many hundreds of careers open to high school students had been adequately studied to identify with confidence the patterns of aptitudes required for success.

As we shall see in the next chapter, the design for Project TALENT calls for studying nearly half a million young people and for follow-up studies regarding their education and careers stretching into the 1980's. Such a design, we believe, should provide us with sharper definitions of talent than we have ever had before — in war or in peace.

4

How can talent be developed?

In the United States we maintain not one but several agencies for the development of talent. Industry with its on-the-job training and apprentice programs; the armed services and their far-reaching training activities; adult education, carried on through formal classes as well as informal arrangements such as public libraries — these are educational agencies of no small import. But it is the public and private schools and colleges to which Americans look first for the development of talent in their youth.

To the public schools we have assigned, at least in principle, no less a goal than helping each child and youth to realize his potential. Here is a goal staggering in its implications. The stated ideal is to leave no one without the benefits of education; to deprive no one of the opportunity to become the kind of happy and productive person he is capable of becoming. Even though few assert that we are within reach of this objective, the people's faith in public education continues to be strong.

America's devotion to the public schools can be measured by two criteria: the support we provide for them; and our readiness to engage in controversy about their aims and practices. Although many observers insist, with justification, that more money must be assigned for public education, we cannot overlook the fact that during 1960, elementary and secondary schools received $16.5 billion. This contrasts with only $6.5 billion just ten years earlier, in 1950. This increase of more than 150% can be compared with an enrollment increase of 45%. Perhaps it is this bite into the taxpayer's dollar that leads citizens to make many demands upon the schools and to criticize them vigorously, and sometimes irresponsibly, when they think their children are not getting full benefit from the tax dollars paid for education.

The public schools have been the center of controversy, raging with various degrees of intensity, for more than 100 years. In our time, the secondary school bears the brunt of unprecedented attacks. Certain academicians assert that basic skills and "hard" subject matter content are being neglected, especially in the training of the superior student. They maintain that in the effort to educate everybody, secondary schools are sacrificing academic standards. Academicians also argue that the secondary schools spend too much time on courses in driver education, courses in personal grooming, and extra-curricular activities. They decry what they claim to be a leveling down of opportunities for the superior mind in favor of turning out "life-adjusted whole children in a common mold." One of their major demands is that the secondary school teachers must have a firmer grounding in subject matter, even if this has to be done at the expense of courses in educational methods.

In reply, the teachers, school administrators (and professors of education!) charge that the academicians would ignore everything but the talents of the college-bound student. They insist that the secondary school program must be suited to all of the types of students enrolled. Secondary education, they assert, must be flexible if the needs of all students are to be met. Nevertheless, sensitive to the academicians' objectives, school officials keep revising and reconstructing the curriculum.

Whether the charges and counter-charges advance the cause of education is doubtful. Equally uncertain is whether "crash" efforts in subject-matter revision, or even carefully planned curriculum innovations, will raise the quality of education. For example, secondary schools are experimenting with two approaches to the "new mathematics." Do these represent an improvement over traditional methods? Schools are also introducing changes in physics, foreign languages, and English. Are these merely changes or do they represent sound educational progress? Such questions are of vital importance to school administrators and to the public. Mere innovations can be differentiated from real improvements only if the results are evaluated over a period of time.

The academicians defend their subject matter areas in a loud and firm voice. No less loud and firm are the voices of those who advocate more and better guidance for children. Much is claimed for guidance. Its advocates insist that if every school were staffed with "an adequate number of well-trained guidance counselors" (though criteria for determining quantity or quality are lacking) we would have less juvenile delinquency, better adjusted children, more intelligent career and scholastic choices, and so on. But to what extent do school guidance activities make a difference in the lives of young people? From where do the influences which shape the lives and careers of young people really come — from classroom teachers, counselors, parents, or the neighbors next door? We do not have the facts to answer such questions. Nor do counselors have scientifically devised tools to appraise vocational fitness. Batteries of tests for some few specific occupations do exist. Some are adequate, some are not. But taken together, these do not begin to cover the occupations found in American industry, business, and the professions.

Speakers in state legislatures and at school board meetings frequently demand the abolition of small schools on the assumption that "the larger the school, the better its education." How do they know? Such speakers rely on the arguments of partisans rather than on the evidence of investigators. We still don't have facts that would answer with precision what effect the size of the school has on the effectiveness of education. Nor do we have evidence to answer a host of other questions. Take these two: To what extent would an increase in appropriations for instruction result in an increase in teaching quality? And, what is the effect of home background and parent occupation on a child's learning?

Although the air in the educational community is thick with expressions of opinion, only rarely is objective proof available to show that one practice is better than another; one policy more productive than a second.

Research studies, designed to make the schools more effective, are under way in many graduate schools and are being sponsored here and there by professional or special-interest groups. But much research in education is limited to surface problems and too few cases. Research also suffers from short-span inquiries.

No single research effort, regardless of scope or duration, can provide all, or even a substantial part, of the information needed for the development of talent in a country as large as ours. Without anticipating what is to follow, we can say now that Project TALENT involves the largest number of school children ever to take part in a research study — and that they will be involved for more than two decades — thus providing the vast dimensions required for an investigation of such complex problems.

5

How can an individual make the best use of his talents?

What does it avail a person if he has a unique pattern of aptitudes and if these are developed — if he doesn't use them? Use of talent is a test of talent. Production is the pay-off. But what forces release our productivity? And how can the levels of productivity be raised so that what we do is more than ordinary or routine, and reaches the quality of creativeness and brings us lasting satisfactions?

Now we are at the last of the three underlying questions about talent — that is, how can the individual best use his talents? Enough research has been done to suggest that there exist forces within us and outside us that can operate on our will to perform and increase our power to create. The research literature on motivation, productivity, and creativity is growing. We shall have occasion to refer to it — in later reports coming from Project TALENT. Some of it is significant and revealing.

For the moment, it will be more revealing to become acquainted with a high school student we shall call Robert. Robert is one of nearly 440,000 students taking part in our research activities. We are not using his real name so we can tell you freely a good deal about him.

When Robert took the Project TALENT tests, he was 16 years old and at the end of his junior year in high school. He reported that he gets up at 5 o'clock every morning to deliver papers. With this and other jobs, he works about 16 to 20 hours a week, earning all his spending money. When he gets home after school, he puts in some time on chores, amounting to about 10 hours a week. Athletics take up 12 hours a week. He also spends part of his spare time building and repairing electrical and electronic apparatus.

He has had four semester courses in science, two in a foreign language, six in social studies, six in English, and six in mathematics. His grades in mathematics have been mostly C's and D's, while his grades in other subjects have been mostly B's and C's. He spends only one to four hours per week on his homework. It appears to be crowded out by other activities and interests (26 to 30 hours of work and 12 hours of athletics each week).

Robert says he likes to hunt, swim, and explore. He does not like to read novels, but he enjoys science fiction and technical books. He states that he would like to work at a government rocket proving ground because he likes working with electricity and electronics.

We have additional facts about Robert which only a battery of aptitude tests similar to that of Project TALENT could reveal. (Figure 1 shows the profile of his test scores.) He had a perfect score on our aeronautics and space information test. He had exceptionally high scores on tests which measured his accumulation of facts on physical sciences and mechanics, his ability to visualize in two dimensions, and his creativity. These high scores suggest that Robert has considerable aptitude in the general field of science. He has probably acquired information about science and mechanics outside the classroom — just as he has confirmed his strong interests in science through spare time tinkering and science-fiction reading.

Our tests also spotlighted an almost hidden fact about Robert. He made a very good score on a math information test, showing that he has considerable general knowledge about mathematics even though his performance in school math work has been below average, as shown by his C and D grades. On the Project TALENT math achievement test his score exceeded those of 78 per cent of the high school juniors in the study — not outstanding, but better than his grades would suggest.

Robert's English test scores were very low. Since a passing grade in English is still one of the requirements for admission

FIGURE 1

Robert's Profile Chart

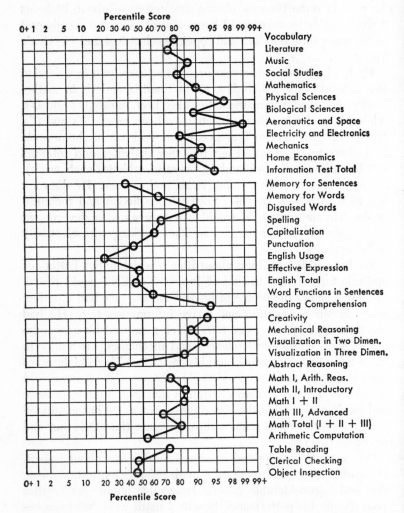

Percentile Score

to colleges and engineering schools, he does not, to the traditional-minded teacher, look like good college material. What are Robert's college plans? He reported to Project TALENT that he might not go to college, although he would like to. He may have to borrow money to do so. If he is able to raise the money, he would like to major in physical science.

Such are the facts Project TALENT obtained about Robert. How can Robert's school and parents use these facts to help him make the best use of his talents?

Teachers could do much to assist in developing Robert's considerable talents in science if they gained an appreciation of the nature of these talents. Once they gain this appreciation (in this instance, from the test scores), they can direct Robert to further education in the physical sciences, since that is what his interests and aptitudes point to. But low math and English grades stand in the way. His teachers, therefore, should try to point out to him the relation of better achievement in math and English, his poor subjects, to physical sciences, his main interest. This encouragement may motivate Robert to study math and English harder. Motivation for Robert can also operate in another way. It is quite possible that the pull of his strong interest in the field of electronics may, itself, induce him to work harder on math and English — that is, if he sees the relationship between these subjects and the job he wants in the future.

Within a year after his graduation from high school, we shall know more about what happened to Robert. We shall ask him to give us facts about his post high school experiences. We shall know whether he has, in fact, enrolled in a college and has chosen the physical sciences as his major interest. Within five years we shall know what kind of employment he has accepted; within ten years we shall know much about his success; and within twenty years we shall know even more about the way in which Robert has used his talents.

Throughout our follow-up of Robert, we shall try to determine how he has utilized his latent talents in the physical sciences; we shall try to identify the educational and occupational experiences which may have encouraged or discouraged his productivity or his creativity. If he is relatively unproductive, we shall try to find the reasons. If, on the other hand, he becomes a highly productive, perhaps creative, person, gaining recognition as scientist or inventor, we shall learn from Robert's record — along with the records of thousands of other students — facts that will help Martha, Peter, and John toward greater productivity and creativity.

2   A Design
for Investigation

Research — "pure" and "applied" — has provided modern man with the means for unlocking nature's secrets and for placing new power in his hands. In this chapter we describe the factors essential to good research and the way in which research methods can be applied to the problems of developing human ability.

We then describe how the research was designed to provide facts to help in bringing about more effective use of talents in scores of occupations. We list some questions about the American high school which require answers. These questions deal primarily with the ways the American secondary school can improve its service to youth — both in the classroom and in the counselor's office.

The year was 1959. In a conference room in the nation's capital, a group of men sat quietly making plans, the final outcome of which would not be felt until 1980. While the headlines shouted threats of atomic war, atmospheric pollution, and Big Brother dictatorship, this group with a more positive and far-sighted approach was outlining the procedures for a long-range, scientific study of American youth and their schools.

In the group were educators, psychologists, and sociologists.

For nearly two years they had been meeting in other conference rooms and other cities in an effort to design the study which to us, on the staff of Project TALENT, was pressing and overdue. These planning meetings were to continue for nearly another year until the blueprint for research procedures was finally completed.

2

If there is a single label to describe the particular educators, psychologists, sociologists and others engaged in this work, the story of which we're about to trace, that label is *behavioral scientist*. As such, they were hard-headed men. And, though they had different interests and backgrounds, they all had been trained in the toughest of all disciplines — the discipline of scientific research.

Scientific research has been defined in many ways — but one thing it is not: it is not burrowing in a library, reading yellowed tomes, or recording the opinions of authorities. Legitimately, however, the term has been stretched to cover many phases of man's inquisitive and inventive activities. There is research in the natural sciences and in the social sciences; there is basic and applied research. Drawing on the results of basic research, industry spends four cents out of every dollar for applied research and for the development of inventive ideas into products. Government, the military, medicine, aviation, forestry — all invest heavily in research. Many observers complain that executives and officials tend to favor "practical" research over "basic" research. There is some justification for the complaint. We don't always recognize that the man who thinks must come before the man who turns that thinking into a product.

Research, fundamentally, is a way of thinking — and out of it come new theories, new knowledge, new products — all equally important. It is thinking based on the observation of many facts. This does not exclude dreaming or formulating hunches. Imagination and hypotheses are important ingredients of research. But above all, the researcher calls for evidence. Observations give us the first approximation to knowledge. The scientist's way of looking and observing must differ from that of the poet — and this without disparaging the latter.

The scientist uses tools to increase the precision of his observations. For the natural scientist such devices may include the microscope or chemical analysis. For the social scientist, they may include interviews, records of experience, test scores, and coefficients of correlation.

As the researcher observes the facts, he records them, classifies them, and sifts the important from the unimportant. Even while he is engaged in these preliminary steps, his mind is already trying to understand what the facts imply — for facts, in themselves, have little value for the researcher or for man in general. Only as facts are analyzed and as generalizations are drawn from them which give us new insights into nature's ways does the researcher feel rewarded. It is here that the researcher faces the most difficult part of his task. This is the phase that demands logical thinking. Reasoning must be applied — reasoning that originates with the observation of particular facts and goes on to a generalization; the thinking frequently involves a shrewd guess — then a return to the facts to search for support or rejection of that guess.

Fact-gathering, fact-analysis, fact-interpretation — these are the trinity of research.

The process and machinery of both basic and applied research have become complicated and mechanized. This has tended to obscure the fact that the underlying force of research is intellectual power. Research begins in the mind. It is the puzzled mind, the curious mind, and the concerned mind which impel men to reach for new knowledge and to seek solutions to men's problems.

3

The behavioral scientists who were helping us lay plans for research into youth's potentialities shared our deep concern over the waste of human abilities, the efficiency of America's education in developing these abilities, and their later utilization for the good of the individual and our country.

These problems stemmed from life. Their solutions had to be sought in life. They could not be found in laboratory settings, through using a few cases under short-term observation. This was especially true of the question of first concern to us and the scientists with whom we were consulting. This question was: How can people make the most of the abilities and aptitudes with which they are endowed?

The aptitude tests developed during World War II had already proved it was possible to devise tests that would predict whether a man could become a successful pilot, navigator, or bombardier. The scores of such tests had provided important clues in assigning military personnel to training in which they would succeed and to jobs in which they would utilize their aptitudes to best advantage. If it were possible to do this for a limited number of wartime occupations, with considerable savings of military manpower, would it not be possible to do it for a larger number of civilian occupations?

We assumed that it would be possible. If so, the subsequent conservation of talent would be enormous. Our assumption was bolstered by postwar research which had centered on the development of aptitude classification tests for a number of civilian occupations. Now we were ready for a bold design which would embrace performance in college and in some hundreds of careers within many occupational fields. Some of the career fields for which partial information was already available are listed in Figure 2.

To develop instruments that would predict a person's performance in these, and other careers, was a venture of no small size. For success, it would require testing large numbers of youth at about the time they were making their first decisions regarding their future careers, and then observing them closely for years — at least until they reached the peak of their productivity. Boys and girls in Grades 9 through 12 clearly provided the best group with which to work on this long-range problem; and while we knew we could not involve all these students, we were convinced that we would require thousands upon thousands of them.

But we required something more — time. Long periods of time. Time in which to observe whether the clues provided by the tests in 1960 were really indicative of how successfully people would be utilizing their aptitudes and abilities in 1961, 1965, 1970, and 1980. The concept of the follow-up was, therefore, incorporated into the design of the research.

We decided to follow up each class of students by mail ap-

FIGURE 2

Some Career Fields for Which Project TALENT Tests May Predict Future Performance

ACCOUNTING

Auditor, Certified Public Accountant, Comptroller, Cost Accountant, Public Accountant, Statistician, Tax Accountant

ENGINEERING AND PHYSICAL SCIENCES

Engineer, Physicist, Chemist

BIOLOGICAL SCIENCES

Agricultural Biologist, Animal Scientist, Plant Scientist, Parasitologist, Entomologist, Hydro-biologist, Biochemist, Biophysicist, Physiologist, Microbiologist

TEACHING

Elementary and High School Teachers

FOREIGN LANGUAGE

Language Specialist, Interpreter, Linguist, Language Teacher, Foreign News Correspondent, Translator

WRITING, JOURNALISM

Journalist, Reporter, Editor, Author, Public Relations Man, Technical Writer, Ad Writer

ART

Architect, Advertising Artist, Illustrator, Industrial Designer, Fashion Designer, Fabric Designer, Lithographer, Painter, Interior Decorator, Engraver

SECRETARIAL

Secretary, Stenographer, Typist, Court Reporter

OFFICE CLERK

Office Clerks: Accounting, Banking, Billing, Correspondence, Filing, Mail, Payroll, Shipping, Statistical, Stock, Receptionist, and others

MECHANICAL WORK

Machinist, Tool and Die Maker, Sheet Metal Worker, Molder, Boilermaker, Automobile Mechanic, Aircraft Mechanic, Machine Repairman, Engine Mechanic, Patternmaker, Welder, Joiner, and others

ELECTRICAL AND ELECTRONICS

Electrician, Electronics Mechanic, Field Service Engineer (electronics), Maintenance Engineer (electronics), TV and Radio Repairman, TV and Radio Studio Engineer, Telegraph and Telephone Electrician

AGRICULTURAL

Farmer, Forester, Horticulturist, Nurseryman

AIRPLANE PILOT

Commercial Pilot, Test Pilot, Instructor Pilot, and others

proximately one year after graduation from high school. Thus, the 12th grade group would be followed up in the summer of 1961; the 11th grade group in 1962; the 10th grade group in 1963; and the 9th grade group in 1964. We also decided to attempt follow-ups five, ten, and twenty years after graduation.

During each of the follow-ups, the individuals will be asked many questions, but mainly they will be asked to report on the training courses and occupations they actually entered, the reasons for their choice, and their success and satisfaction with the activity they chose. By comparing the replies with the original test scores and background data on each student, we will be able to tell how well the tests of 1960 predicted success in the careers chosen by these young people. If the tests and test scores are really effective in predicting success for the activities for which they were designed, then, in time, we shall have instruments of great potential value for the classification and placement of young men and women in tasks which they will ultimately find satisfying and productive.

4

A century and a half ago the United States originated an educational institution which has remained unique in the world. It is the American public secondary school. The Boston Latin Grammar School was the first, and its purpose was to develop the talents of boys planning to enter the ministry, law, or possibly merchandising.

Fifteen decades of growth and change have created a vast network of some 26,000 institutions open to every adolescent, regardless of sex, race, or economic status. Over the years, the high school has adopted philosophies, practices, and offerings appropriate for each generation; some of these have been outgrown, in due time, in favor of newer philosophies, practices, and offerings. Vestiges of the old have always remained. As a result, it is unsafe, today, to generalize about the American high school. Many an institution is a mixture of the traditional and the progressive; of the rigidly academic and the practical life-adjustment type of curriculum. Some high schools spend as little as $140 per pupil; others, more than $500. Some maintain faculties of superbly trained men and women; others are forced to employ teachers with substandard certificates. Some are venturesome, experimenting with new math, Saturday-morning science, teaching teams, and teaching machines. Others are static.

Within the past generation nearly all high schools have been exposed to programs of guidance. Some institutions have established extensive guidance and counseling departments and have supported them with ample funds and administrative encouragement. Other schools have either not been convinced of the value of guidance or have not had the means to create a program that would effectively reach the lives of their pupils. The result is that today American high schools provide guidance services which range from excellent to poor. Some are intensive, others superficial; some are continuous, others hit-or-miss; some are staffed by trained men and women, others by overworked classroom teachers.

Despite the great diversity in character and quality of the secondary school instruction and guidance, all American high schools are pretty much on the same time schedule. Each year they accept an entering class of a few students or a few hundred students — and four years later, willy-nilly, for better or for worse, send about three-fourths of them on either toward post high school education or toward jobs. The remaining quarter drops out before graduation.

What effect do the varied and different high school policies and practices have on the youth? And, specifically, what effect do they have in developing students' innate aptitudes and abilities? We decided to undertake to answer at least the following ten questions:

1. Does the size of a high school make any appreciable difference in the development of youth's talents?

2. Is a high school which spends more money for each of its pupils more efficient in developing men and women who are successful in applying and utilizing their aptitudes?

3. Are small classes more effective than large classes?

4. Is the graduate from a high school with a traditional curriculum more likely to succeed in college than one from a high school with an "activity" curriculum?

5. Does strict discipline within a school have any effect in reducing delinquency and crime rate among its graduates?

6. What factors and forces within a high school operate to hold its pupils until graduation? Conversely, what operates to pull students out before graduation?

7. What is the exact nature of a guidance program which has a deep and lasting effect upon youth in their choice of educational or occupational careers?

8. Which of the many curricular innovations attempted in secondary schools contribute most effectively to success in college work or in paid employment?

9. What effect does the parent's occupation and home background have upon the acquisition of knowledge and development of aptitudes among the young?

10. What is the exact nature of an educational guidance program which helps the student solve his personal problems effectively and develop sound habits, plans, and goals?

These are some of the major questions about schools which we proposed that our research answer. At the same time, we took care to design the study so that a multitude of additional questions could be answered with a precision heretofore impossible.

The gains from a broad evaluation of patterns of aptitudes and abilities will benefit future students. Ten and twenty years from now, young people will be able to study the experiences of thousands of students who left high school between 1960 and 1963 with combinations of aptitudes and abilities similar to their own. They will be able to plan much more wisely for the full development and use of their potential aptitudes and abilities. And the high school of a decade or two hence will also have a body of facts to suggest how educational and guidance programs might be changed to cut the waste of potential talent.

5

Facts. Facts. Facts. Every part of the design for the research called for an unprecedented volume of information about students and their schools. As it turned out, we laid plans to collect about 2,000 items of information about each student and 1,000 items of information about each school. Such a vast amount of data, we hoped, would satisfy the research needs not only of Project TALENT, but also of many other researchers. It became part of our design, therefore, to develop a storehouse of facts for the use of investigators seeking solutions to other pressing educational and manpower problems.

How we gathered these facts, what they cover, how we shall analyze them, and finally, how they will be utilized for the benefit of youth, schools, and the country is the rest of our story.

3

Selecting the
Students and the Schools

A school in Eastern Kentucky, another in the Bronx, and another in Washington, D.C., were among the 1,353 schools taking part in our study. Here we tell how we chose the schools and how we chose the students within the schools for participation in our research.

We describe the scientific way of choosing a random sample of schools and pupils to make sure that all parts of the United States and all sizes and types of schools are fairly represented. We show the number of public, private, and parochial schools taking part in our research, and indicate the states in which they are located.

There is a school in the mountains of Eastern Kentucky which can be reached only by a gravel road bounded on either side by steep hills heavily wooded with pine. Occasionally the woods open sufficiently to reveal a cabin with an out-building, then the trees close in again, the steep slopes silently hostile to attempts to use the land for a livelihood. At a sharp fork in the road, one turns to the right and the road dribbles out and is no more. A wide shallow brook outlines the foot of the hill directly ahead. Across the brook are a school and accompanying dormitories.

The dormitories are necessary, for the isolated and rugged country makes daily trips to and from school impossible. This is the Red Bird Settlement School.

At the corner of West 205th Street and Golden Avenue in the Bronx, New York City, students gather from all over the city to study calculus and advanced courses in science. A high proportion of them will eventually earn doctoral degrees and assume key positions in science. This is the Bronx High School of Science.

Off a residential street in Washington, D.C., a driveway sweeps into a broad arc up a hill in front of the main entrance of a modern parochial secondary school. The structure is of contemporary brick-and-glass design. The school appears to convey an impression of a quiet and efficient atmosphere. Students move from room to room with a bearing which seems to reflect their pride in the physical plant itself. This is the Archbishop Carroll High School.

About the middle of November, 1959, the superintendents responsible for these three schools opened their mail and read a letter inviting them to participate in Project TALENT. Almost a thousand other superintendents received a similar letter at about the same time.

How were the Red Bird Settlement High School, Bronx High School of Science, Archbishop Carroll High School and the other high schools selected for an invitation to join in the project? Who made the decisions, and on what basis? Furthermore, why were not all high schools in the United States invited to take part?

To answer the last question first, only rarely is a research study based on information gathered from 100 per cent of the individuals in a group. Most surveys carried out by the Bureau of the Census, Bureau of Labor Statistics, or Department of Agriculture select only a part of a group to study — sometimes a very small part. In business and industry, too, decisions as to whether a product meets the standard are usually based on inspection of a small proportion of the total output.

Similarly, Project TALENT could not involve all the millions of students enrolled in America's public and private secondary schools. Nor would that be necessary. It was necessary, however, to select a segment of the high school population sufficiently ample in number and so typical in character that we could say —

this portion truly represents the whole. To put it differently, we had to select an adequate and representative sample. To select such a sample, sound methodology is all-important. Nothing could be left to chance — and somewhat paradoxically, this meant that the final choice *had* to be left to chance. If this remark seems enigmatic, we hope later parts of the chapter will clear up the enigma.

2

We decided that a sample involving five per cent of the high school enrollment, or between 400,000 and 500,000 students, would be large enough to provide a sturdy base for our contemplated research structure. Such a sample had the dimensions to satisfy many research needs of the present and future. For one thing, we knew that we would be studying many different groupings and sub-groupings of individuals and schools. To do this adequately, the initial size of the sample had to be large enough so that it could be divided, subdivided, then divided again and still yield substantial information. Later, as follow-up studies progressed, the original facts collected would be broken down for students who did and did not go to college; for those who did and did not finish college; for students who trained for many different professions and occupations; for those who succeeded and those who failed in their chosen field; for those who achieved high standing and renown — and, at the other end of the scale, for those who ran into trouble with society.

But there is still another reason the sample needed to be so large. We knew that a good percentage of this number would go into clerical jobs, sales work, mechanics; a smaller percentage would become lawyers, doctors, nurses, and teachers. But few indeed would become nuclear physicists, research chemists, or theoretical mathematicians. Yet, we would want to trace the factors in the career development of these future high-level specialists. Out of a half million students, probably no more than 2,000 would become Ph.D.'s; of these there might be 100 mathematicians and 200 physicists. A large sample would be necessary if we were to draw these future specialists into our study.

Another question that had to be settled was whether to choose the sample on the basis of school systems, separate schools, or individual students. In many of the studies to be carried out with Project TALENT data, the schools would be the focus of concern. Student achievement and future success would be studied in relation to large and small schools, public and private schools, conventional and experimental curricula, and so on. For this reason — as well as for the sake of administrative efficiency — we established the school as the sampling unit.

How many schools would we need in order to draw a sample consisting of five per cent of high school students? Five per cent of the schools? Theoretically, yes — and, as it turned out, we did give the tests in approximately one out of every twenty schools. But it wasn't as simple as that.

The sizes of public high schools differ radically — from less than a hundred students to more than 5,000. The small high schools dotting the rural countryside are far more numerous than very large city high schools. To emphasize the contrast, the total enrollment of several dozen rural schools may fall far below the enrollment of one city school. To select one out of every 20 schools in the country without consideration of size differences would have resulted in so few large public high schools — and so very many small schools — that our later research on the effects of school size would have been inconclusive. The solution was to invite one out of every 20 medium-sized public high schools to participate in the study; one out of every 13 very large schools; and one out of 50 small schools. We invited one out of 20 private and parochial schools, regardless of size, to participate in Project TALENT.

To adjust for these variations, our statistical procedures called for "weighting" the schools in the analysis of the data obtained from them. Only by applying appropriate weights to the data can results be obtained which permit sound inferences about the total population of high schools or high school students.

3

The decisions made so far controlled the dimensions of the sample to be selected, but they did not control exactly which schools were to be included.

From various sources, primarily the U.S. Office of Education, we had obtained the names and addresses of all high schools in the United States — some 26,000 schools — along with their enrollment figures. It was from these official sources that we had to select approximately one out of every 20 schools. But which ones? We were face to face with the sampling problem.

In order to avoid biases, it is necessary to select the sample in a random manner. A characteristic of a simple random sample is that every member of an entire group has an equal chance of being in the sample. The laws of chance operate in such a way that a random sample will tend to be representative in all respects of the group as a whole.

Random sampling can be improved by a procedure known as stratified random sampling. This consists in dividing the entire group into smaller groups, according to one or more characteristics, and then using a strictly random selection method within each classification. To classify, or "stratify," the total group according to certain characteristics before drawing the random sample makes it more representative in certain respects and less representative in none. In view of this admirable feature, stratified random sampling was the method used in selecting schools to participate in Project TALENT.

There is a limit, of course, to the number of characteristics that can be singled out for such special handling, even in a survey as comprehensive as Project TALENT. We wanted to select only the most important characteristics and through stratifying, take out insurance, so to speak, that the sample would be truly representative in regard to these characteristics.

The first important characteristic to be singled out was an obvious one involving the type of school — public, parochial, or private. In our groupings we included all Roman Catholic high schools in the parochial classification. Other church-affiliated schools were put in the private school group.

We also wanted to be certain that we would have proper geographical representation. There is a big difference in schools because of differences in the economy of the region and the nature of the population. There are also differences in schools because the various state departments of education set different requirements for curricula, teacher certification, and graduation. Still another significant factor is whether the school is in a very large city or a relatively small community. For these reasons, we first grouped schools into broad geographical areas and then sub-grouped them by states, our basic geographic unit. Five cities, because of their large size, were also considered as basic geographic units. These were New York, Chicago, Los Angeles, Philadelphia, and Detroit. Such treatment assured us of having proper large city representation. The map in Figure 3 illustrates the geographical distribution of schools selected to participate in the project. Table 1 shows the number of schools included in each geographical unit.

We next took steps to insure that the sample would reflect the differences in school size. Size is certainly one of the most important variables among schools. For one thing, a small school cannot offer as varied a curriculum as a large school except at greater cost per pupil. We therefore divided the public high schools into the following four groups according to Grade 12 enrollment: (1) those with less than 25 seniors; (2) those with 25-99 seniors; (3) those with 100-399 seniors; (4) those with 400 or more seniors. One reason for this particular division was to set up two groups that would, and two that would not, meet the minimum size standards for schools recommended by educational authorities.

Another characteristic singled out for special attention among public high schools was the student holding power of the schools. In some schools many students drop out before graduation; in others nearly all stay to graduate. Since we assume that there are major differences between schools with high and low holding power, we wanted to be sure we had proper representation of each type. This stratification was made by computing a retention ratio for each school. The ratio was the number of students who graduated in 1958 to the number of students in the 10th grade in 1959. This information provided a separation of schools into categories on the basis of whether (at one end of the scale) nearly all students graduate, or whether (at the other extreme) very few students graduate.

The machine that did the actual selection work (IBM-650) was given considerable human prompting on how to make a random choice from each category. For instance, the machine was instructed to take into account the different sampling ratios that had been set up for schools of different sizes. Instead of picking one in 20 as for medium-sized schools, the machine was

FIGURE 3

The National Sample of Schools

Location of schools selected to participate in Project TALENT

programmed to pick out one out of 13 very large schools and one out of 50 very small schools.

Parochial and private schools were stratified (separately) into the 56 geographical units, but there were too few of these non-public schools to make it desirable to stratify them on school size and holding power, too.

The ninth-grader was, of course, an important individual in our study. But America's public secondary school organization sometimes places the ninth-grader in a four-year public high school and sometimes in a three-year junior high school. Not all graduates of a particular junior high school go to a particular senior high school, and not all tenth-graders in a senior high school come from the same junior high school. This gave rise to complications in obtaining a representative sample of ninth graders. However, a solution to the problem was found. Where junior high schools or groups of junior high schools were clearly and unambiguously associated with a senior high school that had been selected, the ninth-graders in those junior high schools were put in the sample. In communities where the situation was not so clear cut, the coordinators helped in deciding what junior high schools would include the maximum number of ninth-grade students who would go to the selected high school and the minimum number who would go to any other senior high school. A small supplementary sampling of the remaining junior high schools, together with a procedure for adjusting school weights, provided the means for mathematically correcting any minor inaccuracies that might have resulted from the approximation procedure described above for selecting the junior high schools.

One important phase of Project TALENT was to collect information on an entire age group, the 15-year-olds. This meant that the data had to be obtained not only for the 15-year-olds in high schools, but also for 15-year-olds still in Grade 8 or below, already in college, or not in school at all. We decided that the non-high-school 15-year-olds to be included in the study were to be residents of areas served by one-tenth of the public senior high schools selected in the sample. The schools selected in the sampling phase were divided into ten sub-samples which would be as close to equivalent in terms of the stratification variables as could reasonably be achieved. One of these ten sub-samples (designated "Sub-sample 0") was then selected to include the non-high-school 15-year-olds for study. These non-high-school 15-year-olds are not intended to be considered part of the regular sample, which consists entirely of high school students. However, they will supplement the 15-year-olds in the regular sample to provide a picture of the entire age group — the total group of 15-year-old Americans.

Two other special groups require mention at this point. The first consisted of two small groups of schools trying experimental courses in mathematics. The two experimental programs were developed by Dr. Max Beberman of the University of Illinois and Dr. E. G. Begle, formerly of Yale University. The performance of students in this new type of program will be compared with that of matched groups of students who take conventional mathematics courses.

Another special group are the schools in Knoxville, Tennessee, and in the surrounding county, Knox County. Two schools were drawn as part of the regular sample in this area, but as a result of the special interest of the school authorities there it was possible to arrange to test every student in every school — public, parochial, and private — in the entire Knoxville and Knox County area, not only in Grades 9 through 12, but also in Grade 8. This very comprehensive testing in a concentrated area, over a five-grade range, will make possible many special studies that could not otherwise be carried out.

4

Much of the thought, time and effort that went into building the invitation list for Project TALENT would have been in vain if the schools had declined to take part. Our uncertainty on this score was short-lived. When the replies started coming in, they were nearly all in the affirmative. In all, 93% of the schools selected in the sampling process agreed to participate — a surprisingly high percentage in view of the magnitude of the undertaking to which the schools were committing themselves. Table 1 shows the number of schools selected in each part of the country, and the per cent of those which agreed to participate in the project. It should be noted that this table represents only the senior high schools selected *in the sampling process*. It does not

TABLE 1

School Participation in Project TALENT

The number of schools invited and actually participating by geographical units and type of school

Geographical Units PARTICIPATING	Public Senior High Schools			Parochial High Schools			Private High Schools			All Groups Combined			Percent of Schools Participating
	YES	NO	TOTAL	YES	NO	TOTAL	YES	NO	TOTAL	YES	NO	TOTAL	
1. New England	33	–	33	13	–	13	9	–	9	55	–	55	100.0
Maine	6	–	6	1	–	1	2	–	2	9	–	9	100.0
New Hampshire	3	–	3	1	–	1	1	–	1	5	–	5	100.0
Vermont	3	–	3	1	–	1	1	–	1	5	–	5	100.0
Massachusetts	14	–	14	8	–	8	3	–	3	25	–	25	100.0
Rhode Island	2	–	2	–	–	–	–	–	–	2	–	2	100.0
Connecticut	5	–	5	2	–	2	2	–	2	9	–	9	100.0
2. Mid-east	168	8	176	26	5	31	10	3	13	204	16	220	92.7
New York City	85	–	85	3	1	4	2	–	2	90	1	91	98.9
New York (except New York City)	27	4	31	9	–	9	3	–	3	39	4	43	90.7
New Jersey	7	4	11	4	–	4	2	–	2	13	4	17	76.5
Philadelphia	2	–	2	–	2	2	–	1	1	2	3	5	40.0
Pennsylvania (except Philadelphia)	38	–	38	6	2	8	2	1	3	46	3	49	93.9
Delaware	2	–	2	–	–	–	1	–	1	2	–	2	100.0
Maryland	7	–	7	4	–	4	1	–	1	12	–	12	100.0
Dist. of Columbia	–	–	–	–	–	–	–	1	1	–	1	1	0.0

3. Great Lakes	160	5	165	25	2	27	7	1	8	192	8	200	96.0
Ohio	41	1	42	6	–	6	1	–	1	48	1	49	98.0
Indiana	26	–	26	2	–	2	–	–	–	28	–	28	100.0
Chicago	20	–	20	1	2	3	1	–	1	22	2	24	91.7
Illinois (except Chicago)	31	1	32	4	–	4	2	–	2	37	1	38	97.4
Detroit	1	–	1	3	–	3	–	–	–	4	–	4	100.0
Michigan (except Detroit)	22	3	25	6	–	6	2	1	3	30	4	34	88.2
Wisconsin	19	–	19	3	–	3	1	–	1	23	–	23	100.0
4. Plains	112	6	118	16	–	16	5	–	5	133	6	139	95.7
Minnesota	20	–	20	3	–	3	2	–	2	25	1	25	100.0
Iowa	21	1	22	5	–	5	–	–	–	26	1	27	96.3
Missouri	26	1	27	3	–	3	1	–	1	30	1	31	96.8
North Dakota	7	1	8	–	–	–	–	–	–	7	1	8	87.5
South Dakota	9	1	10	1	–	1	–	–	–	11	1	12	91.7
Nebraska	15	–	15	2	–	2	–	–	1	17	–	17	100.0
Kansas	14	2	16	2	–	2	1	–	1	17	2	19	89.5
5. Southeast	216	14	230	13	3	16	8	4	12	237	21	258	91.9
Virginia	14	2	16	1	–	1	1	1	2	16	3	19	84.2
West Virginia	10	1	11	1	–	1	–	–	–	11	1	12	91.7
North Carolina	33	–	33	1	–	1	2	–	2	36	–	36	100.0
South Carolina	15	1	16	–	–	–	–	–	–	15	1	16	93.8
Georgia	19	3	22	1	–	1	–	–	–	20	3	23	87.0
Florida	14	–	14	1	–	1	–	2	2	15	2	17	88.2

(Table continued on next page.)

53

TABLE 1 (Continued)

School Participation in Project TALENT

The number of schools invited and actually participating by geographical units and type of school

Geographical Units PARTICIPATING	Public Senior High Schools			Parochial High Schools			Private High Schools			All Groups Combined			Percent of Schools Participating
	YES	No	TOTAL	YES	No	TOTAL	YES	No	TOTAL	YES	No	TOTAL	
Kentucky	19	—	19	3	1	4	2	—	2	24	1	25	96.0
Tennessee	19	1	20	—	—	—	1	—	1	20	1	21	95.2
Alabama	22	3	25	—	—	—	1	—	1	23	3	26	88.5
Mississippi	14	2	16	2	—	2	—	—	—	16	2	18	88.9
Arkansas	17	1	18	—	1	1	—	—	—	17	2	19	89.5
Louisiana	20	—	20	3	1	4	1	1	2	24	2	26	92.3
6. Southwest	73	7	80	7	—	7	4	—	4	84	7	91	92.3
Oklahoma	21	1	22	1	—	1	1	—	1	23	1	24	95.8
Texas	45	6	51	4	—	4	2	—	2	51	6	57	89.5
New Mexico	5	—	5	1	—	1	1	—	1	7	—	7	100.0
Arizona	2	—	2	1	—	1	—	—	—	3	—	3	100.0
7. Rocky Mountains	24	3	27	2	—	2	2	—	2	28	3	31	90.3
Montana	7	2	9	—	—	—	—	—	—	7	2	9	77.8
Idaho	2	1	3	1	—	1	1	—	1	4	1	5	80.0
Wyoming	2	—	2	—	—	—	—	—	—	2	—	2	100.0
Colorado	9	—	9	1	—	1	—	—	—	10	—	10	100.0
Utah	4	—	4	—	—	—	1	—	1	5	—	5	100.0

8. *Far West*	34	14	48	12	1	13	–	5	5	51	15	66	77.3
Nevada	1	–	1	1	–	1	–	–	–	2	–	2	100.0
Washington	9	1	10	2	–	2	–	2	2	13	1	14	92.9
Oregon	8	1	9	1	–	1	–	1	1	10	1	11	90.9
Los Angeles	2	2	4	1	1	2	–	–	–	3	3	6	50.0
California (except Los Angeles)	14	10	24	7	–	7	–	2	2	23	10	33	69.7
9. *Non-contiguous*	2	–	2	–	–	–	–	1	1	3	–	3	100.0
Alaska	–	–	–	–	–	–	–	1	1	–	–	–	—
Hawaii	2	–	2	–	–	–	–	–	–	3	–	3	100.0
TOTAL	822	57	879	114	11	125	8	51	59	987	76	1063	92.9

include a large number of junior high schools and also many senior high schools in which the tests were administered to supplement the regular sample. Thus the total number of schools shown here as participants is only 987, while testing was actually done in 1,353 schools.

The success of the effort to get an adequately large and adequately representative sample was evident, even on the surface, in the return mail bringing the acceptances of the schools. Letters poured in by the hundreds — from urban schools, suburban schools, and rural schools; from large schools, small schools, and medium-sized schools; from schools in prosperous neighborhoods, and schools in depressed areas; from schools with traditional curricula, and schools with experimental programs; from schools in the East, West, North, and South; from academic high schools, commercial high schools, industrial high schools, and comprehensive high schools.

The gamut, variety, and expanse of America's secondary school system, public and private, were here. But more significantly, letters attested to the readiness of principals and teachers to take part in a study involving close to a half million of the youngsters for whose education and guidance they were responsible.

4
How the
Tests Were Constructed

Why we decided to construct a new battery of tests rather than to use existing tests.

How each item in each test was weighed and analyzed to give our measuring instruments accuracy and precision. We describe the technique of item analysis.

What the final test battery consists of and how many tests it includes.

When a new test battery is to be put together, there are two ways of doing it. One is to select a number of tests from among the many good ones published by commercial and noncommercial agencies. The other way is to develop new tests. After serious consideration we decided not to use ready-made tests. A good battery of tests is not merely a collection of good single tests that happen to be available. A good battery calls for a coordination of tests designed to meet a specific purpose. Central to the purpose of Project TALENT was our aim to survey a variety of human aptitudes and to obtain scores which might predict an individual's ability to develop those aptitudes for vocational and educational success. Such a purpose called for a large number of fairly short tests, rather than a small number of longer tests. While individual scores on longer tests may be more accurate (or to use the technical term, more "reliable"), the composite score from a few long tests will probably give less accurate predictions of vocational and educational success than the composite score from a larger number of shorter tests measuring a greater variety of aptitudes and abilities.

Ready-made tests are often of the longer variety, and in any case, tests that would otherwise be suitable would not likely be the right length for the purposes of this battery. Avoiding unduly long tests was especially important because testing time was considerably limited. We had to make the best use of each test within the short time period at our disposal. Thus, one major advantage of our decision to develop an entirely new battery of tests specifically for Project TALENT was that we could control the length of the tests, making each as long or as short as seemed desirable in order to make the battery as useful as possible for many kinds of predictions.

There were other advantages, too. New tests gave us assurance that none of them had been taken before by any of the students in the study. Further, the tests could be taken out of circulation. Their use in the future could be restricted to studies related directly to Project TALENT, and to calibration studies that establish relationships between the TALENT scores and scores on other standardized tests, so that Project TALENT results can be applied to those tests.

The decision to develop a new battery of tests for Project TALENT set in motion a chain of events beginning with the detailed planning that led to the creation of an experimental battery, and to its refinement into the end-product — the battery of tests finally used.

2

An aircraft or automobile manufacturer does not put his product on the market without first building a model, testing it, and then modifying and improving it on the basis of test flights or road tests. By the same token, we were not planning to subject nearly 500,000 boys and girls to tests without first creating an experimental battery, trying it out, and improving it on the basis of the tryouts.

In developing the experimental battery, we followed these steps:

We reviewed past research and experience in test construction.

We determined the kinds of tests we would build for the experimental battery.

We wrote detailed specifications for each test. Not until then did we write the items, organize them into tests, and organize the tests into a single battery.

We arranged for a tryout in a few schools.

We analyzed the results to decide which of the tests and which of the items to keep in the final products.

Our review of past research gave us many clues as to the kinds of measuring instruments that would be useful for Project TALENT. But we knew we had to work within limitations. First, there was the limit of time. We could not expect the schools to provide more than two days of testing time. Second, the tests had to be of the objective type, not only because of their greater reliability, but also because only tests that could be machine-scored would be practical in testing hundreds of thousands of individuals. Third, most of the tests had to be of reasonably well-established types, because the battery was to be based chiefly on what had been learned over the years about the art of test construction and about the uses of various kinds of tests, rather than on speculation. Most of the tests had to measure abilities, aptitudes, and kinds of achievement which were of demonstrated importance and predictive value. While tests of an experimental nature were not ruled out, they could represent no more than a very small fraction of the final battery.

Before the tests themselves could be written, detailed specifications had to be prepared for them, stating not only the number and kind of items but also the reasons for using items of that type, suggestions for constructing them, characteristics the items should have, and characteristics they should *not* have. On the quality of the specifications depends the quality of the final instruments. If the specifications are well done and if the items are written to conform with the specifications, the test is far more likely to be a good one than if the author dived headlong into writing test items.

Our plans called for a larger number of tests in the experimental form than we expected to use in the final battery, since it was expected that some tests would be eliminated on the basis of the tryout results. In the initial test development stage it was better to err in the direction of too many tests than too few. We decided to develop experimental forms of 29 tests, plus three inventories — an interest inventory, a student activities inventory, and a student information blank. The 29 tests are listed in Figure 4.

FIGURE 4

*Composition of Experimental Test Battery**

1. Vocabulary-Information Profile
2. English: Active Vocabulary
3.   Effective Expression
4.   English Usage
5.   Sentence Structure
6.   Punctuation
7.   Capitalization
8.   Spelling
9. Reading Comprehension
10. Following Directions
11. Disguised Words
12. Words in Sentences
13. Paired Associates
14. Sentence Completion

15. Arithmetic Computation
16. Arithmetic Reasoning
17. Mathematics A. (through Grade 9)
18. Mathematics B. (Grades 10–12)
19. Verbal Reasoning
20. Abstract Reasoning
21. Mechanical Reasoning
22. Spatial A. Folding
23. Spatial B. Rotation-Reflection
24. Scale Reading
25. Name Comparison
26. Table Reading
27. Form Perception
28. Social Judgments

29. Creativity

* A table giving more details about these tests will be found in the Appendix, Section A.

In addition to constructing more tests than we planned to use, we also included more items for each test in the experimental battery than would be needed in the final form. The reason was the same: once the test material was subjected to tryout and analysis, some of the items would necessarily be dropped.

With construction of the experimental battery completed according to the specifications, we were ready for the tryout. This was done in 11 widely separated high schools — large and small; rural, urban, and suburban; and located in the Northeast, South, and Midwest. All students in Grades 9 through 12 were tested — a total of almost 6,000 boys and girls.

The two main purposes of the tryout, then, were: first, to decide what tests were to be included in the final battery and how long they should be; second, to provide a basis for deciding, in the case of those tests that *were* to be in the final battery, which test items should be included. What we needed from the tryouts were the scores that each student made on each of the tests and his response to each item in each test. The information on how each student responded to specific items was especially important to us, for it was this information, analyzed by an electronic computer, which helped us decide which items to retain and which to eliminate from the tests. This process is called "item analysis." Let us become acquainted with it, because the quality of item analysis determines, in part, the quality of the final tests.

3

Item analysis is a statistical process. As such, it can not substitute for judgment and care in writing the items — nothing can. But item analysis can be an invaluable help. Let's see how.

Consider the following general information test item (this is not one we would ever have used):

A mixture of blue and yellow produces
   A. orange
   B. red
   C. green
   D. white
   E. brown

This is a poor test item because it is ambiguous; it has two defensible answers instead of one. The physicist knows that a combination of blue light and yellow light produces white; the artist knows that mixing blue pigment and yellow pigment produces green pigment. Obviously, then, either C or D would be a defensible answer. Now suppose that the author of the item does not know much about physical science and thinks that C is the only answer. He designates C as the answer. The students who know neither about the mixing of pigments nor the mixing of colored light rays will have no idea of the answer. They may guess any of the choices, or they may omit the item. The students who know about pigment-mixing but not about light-mixing will pick C. The other group of students with partial knowledge, those who know about light-mixing but not about pigment-mixing, will pick D. But what about those students who are best informed? They are the ones who will really be puzzled by the item since they may recognize its ambiguity. These students may answer C, or they may answer D, but they are likely to omit the item entirely.

One purpose of an item analysis is to find out what kind of total scores on the test are earned by the students who select each choice on any particular item. The results for the item we have been talking about are likely to be somewhat as follows: The students who pick A, B, or E will have lower total scores on the average than those who pick C or D; but those who omit the item altogether may have the highest scores of all. These results serve as a signal that something is wrong with the item. Another clue might be provided if, as seems likely, the average score of the students who chose D were about as high as the score of those who picked the supposed answer, C. If further delving revealed exactly what the trouble was, the item could be revised and salvaged. For instance, the difficulty could be overcome by changing the item to read as follows:

Mixing blue paint with yellow paint produces
    A. orange paint
    B. red paint
    C. green paint
    D. white paint
    E. brown paint

Then the item would have only one correct answer, C.

Now let us look at another test item. Suppose that the following item were included in a ninth-grade mathematics test:

The value of π is closest to
    A. 3.141588
    B. 3.141589
    C. 3.141591
    D. 3.141593
    E. 3.141594

This is a poor item because it would be ridiculous to require ninth-grade students to memorize the value of π to that many decimal places. It would be unreasonable to expect it even of a professional mathematician. However, if this item did get into a mathematics test, the results for the item analysis no doubt would suggest that good and poor students alike were guessing on the item. Probably about the same number of students would choose each option, and those who chose option D, the correct answer, would not have higher scores on the rest of the test than those who chose A, B, C, or E. This item would undoubtedly be thrown out of the test, since the item analysis would make it immediately apparent that it was too hard. A test item so difficult that practically no one in the group for which the test was intended knows the answer has no place in the test. Similarly, item analysis results can point out items that are too easy.

We analyzed each response to each item in the TALENT experimental battery. For each response we computed (with the help of machines) the per cent of students reaching the item who selected that response, the average score achieved by them on the test, and an index[1] which indicates the degree to which students who picked the response in question tend to have higher (or lower) scores than students who picked other responses for the same item.

The same kinds of data were obtained for students who reached an item but deliberately omitted it as for those who picked a specific option. Thus omission of an item was treated as what it really is — a form of response.

The entire item analysis was carried out separately for the lower grades (Grades 9 and 10) and for the upper grades (Grades 11 and 12).

These statistical procedures yielded values which guided us in retaining, revising, or rejecting specific items.

One additional value was obtained for each item — the per cent of students reaching it. Again this was done separately for the upper grades and the lower grades. These percentages provided a basis for deciding on the time limits for the tests, or alternatively for deciding on the number of items appropriate for a given time limit.

Item analysis provided the basis for revising experimental forms of tests to produce final forms of the tests that were to be included in the final battery. But the item analysis alone was

[1] Statisticians call this a "point biserial correlation coefficient."

not a good basis for deciding whether a test should be included. Other facts were needed for that decision. The main problem here was efficient use of testing time. We wanted the final battery to consist of tests that would measure as many different things as possible and overlap each other as little as possible. We wanted each test to be adequately reliable and at the same time we wanted to make certain that each test would make a unique contribution to the battery. How this was done (see Appendix, Section B) is of more interest to the expert than to the lay reader. What needs to be recorded here is that on the basis of consideration of the available facts, we decided to eliminate four tests that were in the experimental battery, revise a few tests substantially, and make only minor revisions in most of the others.

We also decided to allot five minutes apiece for each of two very brief themes to be written by the students. These themes were to be on the topics, "What High School Means to Me" and "My Views About an Ideal Occupation."

4

After the general decisions had been made as to content of the final battery, one decision still remained before the tests could be revised and organized into a single, integrated battery. This was the question of how the various parts of the battery were to be handled in the initial phase of the data processing.

It seems advisable to anticipate Chapter 11 at this point by indicating that two different kinds of machines — a "scoring machine" and a "document reader" — were available for use in the initial processing. These are described in detail in Chapter 11. At this point it will suffice to say that the scoring machine, as its name implies, yields "scores" on sets of items. The document reader, on the other hand, records specific responses without scoring them.

It was decided to arrange the battery so that all of the students' responses would fit on five answer sheets, two of which would be processed on the scoring machine and the remaining three on the document reader. Document reader answer sheets would include the Student Information Blank, the Interest Inventory, and basic information data — student's name, address, sex, date of birth, grade in school. The scoring machine answer sheets would include the Student Activities Inventory and all of the tests except the Information Test. The Information Test posed a problem both because it had so many items and because some of the items were of such a nature that it seemed appropriate to score them individually. The solution was simple. The Information Test was split into two parts. Part I responses would be put on an answer sheet earmarked for the scoring machine; Part II responses would be put on an answer sheet of the type to be processed by the document reader.

Having settled these problems, we were in a position to complete the jigsaw puzzle by combining all the pieces — the tests, three inventories, two themes, and an instrument containing basic identifying information — to form a single, fully organized battery. The composition of the final battery is shown in Figure 5.

FIGURE 5

*Composition of the Final Project TALENT Battery**

APTITUDE AND ACHIEVEMENT TESTS

1. Information Test	12. Creativity
2. Memory for Sentences	13. Mechanical Reasoning
3. Memory for Words	14. Visualization in Two Dimensions
4. Disguised Words	15. Visualization in Three Dimensions
5. English: Spelling	16. Abstract Reasoning
6. Capitalization	17. Mathematics: Arithmetic Reasoning
7. Punctuation	18. Introductory
8. English Usage	19. Advanced
9. Effective Expression	20. Arithmetic Computation
10. Word Functions in Sentences	21. Table Reading
11. Reading Comprehension	22. Clerical Checking

23. Object Inspection

MISCELLANEOUS	INVENTORIES
Preferences Test	Student Activities Inventory
Themes	Interest Inventory
	Student Information Blank

* A table giving details about these tests will be found in the Appendix, Section C.

Physically, the final battery consists of five test booklets and five separate answer sheets. The five test booklets were designated A, B, C1, C2, and C1x. The five answer sheets were designated A, B1, B2, C and Z. Answer Sheet Z is the "Master Record Form" containing the student's name, address, and other identifying information.

After all materials were completed and organized into proper place and sequence, we put the entire new battery to one more trial — a full-scale "dress rehearsal." This took place in February, 1960. The stage was Preston High School, Preston, Maryland, where the full two days of the battery were administered. Since things went smoothly, only a few minor changes in time limits were necessary before the presses could start rolling to turn out materials for the full testing program.

5 The Tests: Their History and Content—1

Here we begin to describe the tests in Project TALENT's battery. This chapter is devoted to a description of the far-ranging Information Test. It includes test items on vocabulary, literature, social studies, mathematics, physical science, biological science, music, art, home economics — and this is but a partial list. The Information Test also measures the student's acquaintance with mechanical, electrical, electronic, aeronautics and space information.

We present sample after sample of test items to show the kinds of questions which the students had to answer.[1] Equally important is the reasoning that went into the building of each phase of the Information Test.

T esting has a long history — probably as long as the history of schools. Standardized objective tests reach back into the late 19th century. They were given their first impetus by such great pioneers as Binet, Galton, and Spearman. In 1897, Joseph M. Rice developed a standardized spelling test and through it demonstrated what he later called the "futility of the spelling grind."

[1] Test items and other material reproduced in this volume from the original battery of Project TALENT tests are used with the permission of the copyright owners, University of Pittsburgh.

From these and other early efforts have come, over the past half century, an increasing number of standardized tests which have steadily improved in effectiveness.

As we in Project TALENT began to develop our battery, we had a vast storehouse of experience to draw on. We reviewed the work of the countless experimenters during the past six decades, so that we could utilize, or adapt to our needs, the best of their ideas, and the principles of test construction that had been arduously developed.

What were the antecedents, characteristics, and contents of the tests we finally laid before the students taking part in our study? Section C of the Appendix summarizes some features of the tests. But the extent and range of the TALENT tests can be better grasped by dividing them into two components — (1) the Information Test, and (2) a group of 17 other tests — measuring many different aptitudes, as well as achievement in several areas. The present chapter deals solely with the first of these components — the Information Test.

2

The Information Test is really several tests rolled into one. Its purpose is multiple. The test may be so scored as to measure the breadth of the student's general information, his vocabulary level, and the amount of information he has in many specific areas. But the test was designed to do much more: to help in identifying mentally retarded students and others who read so poorly as to be considered functionally illiterate; to help us identify students whose attitude toward taking the test is flippant or apathetic and students whose scores may be pulled down by careless errors; finally, to help determine a student's general attitude toward natural phenomena — whether he tends to take a scientific view in evaluating hypotheses, or whether his general attitude makes him receptive to explanations which are superstitious or otherwise illogical.

This is a large assignment for a single test — even one as long as the Information Test. However, many of the items have multiple functions. For example, the items designed to identify illiterates also help to identify the inadequately motivated students — provided that the entire pattern of scores is taken into account and that the results are properly interpreted. And every item, regardless of what else it measures, also contributes to the total "general information" score.

Let's examine more closely each of the purposes for which the Information Test is designed, and the historical background that preceded the development of this test.

1. Measures of breadth of general information. Information tests covering a wide range of topics have been used as components of general intelligence tests as far back as World War I, when the Army Alpha test was given to all recruits who could read and write. One of the eight subtests of the Army Alpha was a test of information, covering a wide range of subject matter. For instance, it included items testing information on animals and birds, physical science, biological science, farming, mechanics, social studies, electricity, medicine, games, business, foods, airplanes, sports, guns, law, literature and art. Arthur S. Otis, who played a leading role in the development of the Army Alpha, later used information items as one of the chief components of his widely used intelligence tests (the Otis Self-Administering Tests of Mental Ability and the Otis Quick-Scoring Mental Ability Tests).

Information tests as indicators of general intelligence have been considered important from the time they were first developed and are still so considered.

2. Measures of interest. In the 1930's there was some experimentation with information and vocabulary tests to measure interest patterns. For instance, there was the Michigan Vocabulary Profile Test, developed by E. B. Greene in 1937. This test consisted of eight subtests, measuring vocabulary in human relations, commerce, government, physical science, biological science, mathematics, fine arts, and sports. The total score on this test provides a measure of general vocabulary. But the innovation which distinguished this test from its predecessors was the recommendation that the profile of subtest scores be used to provide a clue to a person's relative interests in different areas. Such a suggestion was based on the premise that the individual will tend to know a good deal about areas in which he has a deep interest. Thus, if the profile of his subscores shows peaks and valleys, these extremes may be taken to suggest areas where his interests, and thus perhaps his ability to succeed, are greatest and least.

The use of information tests to suggest whether an individual has sufficient interest in an activity to succeed in it was greatly expanded and systematized during World War II in the Army Air Force Aviation Psychology Program. It proved successful in the battery of Aircrew Classification Tests designed to predict success as a pilot, bombardier, or navigator.

A battery later developed by the American Institute for Research to select airline pilots and flight engineers made use of many principles and methods which had proved effective in the Air Force. Among them was the use of information tests to provide an "operational" measure of interest in flying — a measure based not merely on claiming interest, but on demonstration of interest by the acquisition of information. The extent to which knowledge about flying indicates a specialized interest rather than merely the acquisition of a wide range of information can be determined by comparing a flying information score with one based on other information, or with the total information score.

3. *Measures of information in specific areas.* In addition to indicating relative interest in different areas, subscores on a general information test are also useful as direct measures of the amount of information acquired in an area — for instance, physical science, fine arts, or sports. The Michigan Vocabulary Profile Test, which has already been mentioned, provides such scores.

Are such scores measures of achievement, or do they measure aptitude? The answer is, they can measure either, or both, depending on the way the scores are interpreted and used. Acquisition of information in a particular area, such as science, certainly represents a kind of achievement. And, in the sense that past performance predicts future performance, achievement would constitute an index of aptitude. In fact, there are certain areas in which these joint achievement-aptitude tests based on amount of information acquired have proved outstandingly useful as predictors or indicators of job aptitudes. Among the areas to which this would apply are mechanics, electrical and electronic work, and aeronautics. The TALENT Information Test items in these three areas may thus be regarded not only as contributing to the total Information score, but also as constituting important separate tests in their own right. These three areas are discussed separately later in the chapter.

4. *Measures of vocabulary.* The size of a person's general vocabulary has long been recognized as one of the best indices of that aspect of general intelligence called "verbal intelligence." Vocabulary tests have played a role in intelligence testing ever since the Binet scale was developed in 1905. Almost every intelligence test (except those specifically designed to be non-verbal) contains either a vocabulary subtest or vocabulary items scattered throughout the test.

There are more ways to measure a person's vocabulary than by listening to his conversation. Standardized paper-and-pencil tests are a much better way. Vocabulary items can take many forms — such as the following:

a. Verbal analogy items

Item 1. "Hand" is to "gauntlet" as "sword" is to

    A. attack.
    B. armor.
    C. shield.
    D. spear.
    E. scabbard.

(The answer is E.)

b. Opposites items (antonym items)

Directions: Choose the word that is most nearly opposite in meaning to the given word.

Item 2. **Hope**

    A. Dislike
    B. Despair
    C. Wish
    D. Fail
    E. Criticize

(The answer is B.)

c. Synonym items

Directions: Choose the word that has most nearly the same meaning as the given word.

Item 3. **Apparel**

        A. Appearance
        B. Illusion
        C. Luggage
        D. Clothing
        E. Elegance

(The answer is D.)

d. Same-opposite items

Directions: Each item consists of five words. Find the two that are most nearly the *same* in meaning or the *opposite* in meaning.

Item 4.

        A. Adjust
        B. Admit
        C. Adapt
        D. Adept
        E. Advise

(The answer is the pair A and C.)

e. Definition items

Item 5. **Suffrage is the right to**

        A. petition.
        B. vote.
        C. assemble.
        D. worship.
        E. work.

(The answer is B.)

5. *Identification of illiterates and persons with severe reading disabilities.* Among the items in the Information subtest of the Army Alpha were some extremely easy ones, put in to screen illiterates. For instance, one asked whether it was more likely

to snow in winter than in summer; another dealt with the fact that eggs come from hens. Tests developed after the Army Alpha have also used this method to spot illiterates. The usual procedure is to incorporate these simple items with the items of normal difficulty in a single score. It is not customary to obtain a separate score on the extra easy items. However, a separate score on these items was obtained by Project TALENT in an effort to identify students whose reading skills are so inadequate that their scores on the rest of the Information Tests and other tests in the battery would be invalidated by failure to understand the items.

6. Measures of motivational factors.   A poor score on items so easy that anyone who can read and write should be able to answer all correctly usually indicates either illiteracy or a severe reading disability. If these explanations do not fit, the next most probable explanation is that the attitude of the person taking the test leaves much to be desired. Or the low score may be due to flippancy (manifested by deliberately marking the wrong answers) or to apathy and indifference. Another possibility is that the low score may be due to unusual proneness to clerical errors.

Obviously the low score does not come with a label attached telling which is the right explanation. However, reasonably accurate inferences may be drawn on the basis of the entire pattern of the student's scores on the rest of the tests.

7. Measures of scientific attitude.   Interspersed among the items of the Project TALENT Information Test is a new kind of item designed to measure scientific attitude. This is one of the Project's experimental ventures in testing. It will be discussed at the end of this chapter.

3

We are now ready to look more closely at the TALENT Information Test. It consists of 395 items. All of them, with the exception of ten inserted to measure scientific attitude, test factual information. The ten scientific attitude items require a composite of information, scientific attitude, and judgment.

The Information Test was divided into two parts on the basis of whether subscores were to be punched on the Scoring Machine or whether specific item responses were to be punched on the Document Reader. Part I can yield 15 subscores and a score representing the sum of the subscores — that is, 16 scores in all. But potentially the test can yield a very large number of additional scores, since the items in Part II, for which individual responses were punched on the Document Reader, can be combined and recombined in any way desired. They can also be combined in any way with some or all of the 15 subscores obtained in Part I. Thus, scales can be tailor-made for specific purposes and for predicting success in particular occupations. The tailor-made scale can be made by combining whatever test items seem best for the specific purpose.

TABLE 2

Content of Information Test

| | Number of Items | | |
	GENERAL VOCAB.	OTHER	TOTAL
PART I OF TEST*			
1. Screening (of illiterates and others)	–	12	12
2. Vocabulary	21	–	21
3. Literature	–	24	24
4. Music	–	13	13
5. Social Studies	–	24	24
6. Mathematics	–	23	23
7. Physical Science	–	18	18
8. Biological Science	–	11	11
9. Scientific Attitude	–	10	10
10. Aeronautics and Space	–	10	10
11. Electricity and Electronics	–	20	20
12. Mechanics	–	19	19
A. Tools, construction	–	(10)	(10)
B. Motors and mechanisms	–	(9)	(9)
13. Farming	–	12	12
A. Farm	–	(8)	(8)
B. Ranch	–	(4)	(4)
14. Home Economics	–	21	21
A. Cooking	–	(11)	(11)
B. Other	–	(10)	(10)
15. Sports	–	14	14
SUBTOTAL	21	231	252

	Number of Items		
	GENERAL VOCAB.	OTHER	TOTAL
PART II OF TEST**			
16. Art	1	11	12
17. Law	1	8	9
18. Medicine	1	8	9
19. Engineering	–	6	6
20. Architecture	–	6	6
21. Journalism	1	2	3
22. Foreign Travel	–	5	5
23. Military	–	7	7
24. Accounting, business, sales	2	8	10
25. Practical knowledge	–	4	4
26. Clerical	–	3	3
27. Bible	–	15	15
28. Colors	–	3	3
29. Etiquette	–	2	2
30. Hunting	–	5	5
31. Fishing	–	5	5
32. Outdoor activities (other)	1	8	9
33. Photography	–	3	3
34. Games (sedentary)	–	5	5
35. Theater	–	6	6
36. Ballet	1	1	2
37. Foods	–	4	4
38. Miscellaneous	1	9	10
SUBTOTAL	9	134	143
TOTAL	30	365	395

° Fifteen subscores and a total score were obtained on Part I.
°° On Part II individual responses to each item were recorded on punched cards.

Table 2 shows the number of items of each kind that constitute the Information Test. Note the 15 categories in Part I for which subscores were obtained.

4

Let us look at some of the scales which have been constructed from the scores on items included in the Information Test.

Vocabulary. The items of the vocabulary scale in the Information Test are designed to measure a student's general vocabulary.

Although the distinction between general and technical or specialized vocabulary is not precise, general vocabulary can be considered to consist of words that educated persons might reasonably be expected to know, whether they have had specialized training in a particular area or not.

As an example of the type of vocabulary items used, note the following:

Item 6. **Which of these objects is usually spherical?**

    A. A water glass
    B. An orange
    C. A doughnut
    D. A dime
    E. A cone

(The answer is B.)

Item 7. **The government of the United States is called "federal" because it has**

    A. a president.
    B. three separate branches.
    C. free elections.
    D. separate states.
    E. separation of Church and State.

(The answer is D.)

Item 8. **Another word meaning *vapor* is**

    A. water.
    B. gas.
    C. liquid.
    D. condensation.
    E. solid.

(The answer is B.)

The terms *spherical, federal,* and *vapor* represent concepts from mathematics, social studies, and physical science, respectively, but they are also part of a person's general vocabulary. The inclusion of such words is one way (a relatively minor way, perhaps, but nevertheless one that might have interesting results) in which the TALENT vocabulary scale differs from many widely used vocabulary tests which appear to be limited to words of a rather "literary" character. Although the TALENT vocabulary items cover a wider range of words than items in these other tests, still the TALENT items do not include words of highly specialized character — for instance, *binomial* or *apothem* (mathematics terms); *pocket borough, fief* (social studies terms); *halogen, ohm* (physical science terms). Items on such words could legitimately go in the appropriate subject-matter scale, but not in the vocabulary scale, for such terms depend more on specialized training in the particular area than on general level of vocabulary.

The vocabulary score estimates ability to comprehend words, not ability to select and use the appropriate word to express one's meaning. Nor are fine differentiations in meanings a matter of concern. Thus, although the dictionary indicates a slight difference in implication between *questionable* and *doubtful,* the meanings are sufficiently similar that for purposes of the TALENT vocabulary scale the two words can be considered synonymous.

5

In addition to the measure of vocabulary, the Information Test yields a series of subscores measuring a student's acquisition of facts in both academic and non-academic subjects. The test items were so constructed that a pupil's answers would reflect his formal education as well as learning he had acquired outside the classroom through reading, radio, television, browsing, listening, or tinkering.

Literature. The purpose of this scale is to measure the pupil's familiarity with the world of literature. There is no common body of literature to which all high school students are likely to have been exposed. No two lists of required or recommended reading issued by schools are identical. In fact, it is probable that any two such lists would differ considerably. Even so, there is usually considerable overlap. Thus, the broad coverage of the Information Test items dealing with literature makes it likely that students who have acquired the habit of reading will get reasonably good scores — provided their reading is above the comic-book level and not limited to the "how-to-build-it-yourself" type.

In developing the literature scale, we made sure that both poetry and prose were represented, including literature for adolescents and adults as well as children. Emphasis was placed on items to test knowledge that would be acquired chiefly by reading the literary work in question, rather than merely by reading *about* it. Items were included about characteristics of the principal characters, plot, and settings.

The following are sample items:

> *Item 9.* **Which of these was a knight of King Arthur's Round Table?**
>
> > A. Alfred
> > B. Lancelot
> > C. Merlin
> > D. Ivanhoe
> > E. Roland

(The answer is B.)

> *Item 10.* **Othello's motive for murder was**
>
> > A. self-defense.
> > B. jealousy.
> > C. fear.
> > D. craving for power.
> > E. greed for gold.

(The answer is B.)

> *Item 11.* **Each line of blank verse has**
>
> > A.   6 feet.
> > B. 10 feet.
> > C.   3 feet.
> > D.   4 feet.
> > E.   5 feet.

(The answer is E.)

Social Studies. This scale covers facts and concepts from history, economics, government and civics, geography, and current affairs. At least half of the history, government, and geography items are concerned with the United States, but the rest of the world is not neglected. The sampling of material on United States history covers periods from the discovery of America to

the present, and includes political, economic, industrial, and
military developments.

No items that seemed likely to become dated within 20 years
or whose significance seemed likely to change markedly within
that period were included in the test. However, this did not pre-
clude items on topics of current concern which will probably
be of continuing interest for a long time.

Materials not necessarily taught in high school were not rigidly
excluded from the test since it was felt that acquisition of knowledge about such materials through voluntary reading or in other
ways indicates special interest in the area.

The following are sample items:

Item 12. **Which of these is specifically required by the U.S.
Constitution?**

    A. Supreme Court
    B. Political parties
    C. Congressional committees
    D. Nominating conventions
    E. Cabinet

(The answer is A.)

Item 13. **Most of the people of India are**

    A. Moslem.
    B. Buddhist.
    C. Christian.
    D. Confucian.
    E. Hindu.

(The answer is E.)

Item 14. **Napoleon was emperor of France around the beginning
of the**

    A. 15th century.
    B. 16th century.
    C. 17th century.
    D. 18th century.
    E. 19th century.

(The answer is E.)

Mathematics. The area of mathematics, unlike other academic subject matter areas, is represented not only in the Information Test, but in two other Project TALENT tests: the Arithmetic Computation Test and the Mathematics Test.

However, the mathematics items in the Information Test do not overlap the content of these other tests since the Information Test items are concerned with knowledge of facts, not with mathematics skills. None of the Information items requires computation, reasoning, or problem-solving — these processes are covered in other tests. Nearly half of the items are on topics studied in Grade 9 or earlier; the others are concerned with topics usually not touched upon until at least the 10th grade; and some call for information that might be acquired in ways other than through classroom mathematics.

The history of mathematics was not included, since there is some evidence that items of this type are less satisfactory indicators of interest in such an area than items testing knowledge of the current field.

The content sampled includes definitions, the vocabulary of mathematics, conventions of mathematical notation, and the understanding of concepts such as fractions, decimals, percents, factors, equations, planes, angles, logarithms, and exponents.

Sample items follow:

Item 15. "$3b + 2b^2 = 5$" is called

  A. a coefficient.
  B. an equation.
  C. a formula.
  D. an unknown.
  E. an identity.

(The answer is B.)

Item 16. **An ordinary slide rule is designed for**

  A. computing.
  B. measuring length.
  C. measuring angles.
  D. weighing.
  E. reading tables.

(The answer is A.)

Physical science. This scale comprises items from chemistry, physics, astronomy, and other physical sciences. Included were science topics taught in elementary and secondary school, as well as items on information that might readily be acquired in ways other than through formal instruction. It was felt that acquisition of such knowledge through voluntary reading and experimentation would indicate a special interest in the area.

Sample items follow:

Item 17. **Ozone is a form of**

    A. electricity.
    B. air.
    C. oxygen.
    D. nitrogen.
    E. carbon dioxide.

(The answer is C.)

Item 18. **Gravitation is the force which causes a rubber ball to**

    A. bounce.
    B. go flat.
    C. keep its shape.
    D. fall when dropped.
    E. change shape when pressed.

(The answer is D.)

Item 19. **A "light year" is a unit of**

    A. temperature.
    B. volume.
    C. brightness.
    D. distance.
    E. speed.

(The answer is D.)

Biological science. This scale includes items from the fields of botany, zoology, and microbiology. Nature lore is covered because its acquisition would indicate a special interest in one area of the biological sciences.

A sample item follows:

Item 20. **The substance which makes plants green is**

    A. cellulose.
    B. starch.
    C. chlorophyll.
    D. sap.
    E. fungus.

(The answer is C.)

Music. While these items are not indicative of musical talent, those who enjoy going to concerts or listening to music on the radio and phonograph should do well on them.

Here is a sample item:

Item 21. **Who wrote "Peter and the Wolf"?**

    A. Prokofiev
    B. Bach
    C. Tschaikowsky
    D. Dukas
    E. Mozart

(The answer is A.)

Art. This scale measures knowledge about art which may have been acquired through participating in art as a hobby or for personal expression. Those who enjoy going to museums and art galleries, reading about art, and dabbling in it should have an advantage on these items — as should those who have had special training in art. However, there is no reason to think that this scale will identify those with creative talents in art.

Two sample items follow:

Item 22. **Easels are used by**

    A. sculptors.
    B. musicians.
    C. surgeons.
    D. lawyers.
    E. painters.

(The answer is E.)

Item 23. **Which of these is *not* the name of a famous painter?**

    A. Titian
    B. Rubens
    C. Cézanne
    D. Napoli
    E. Van Dyck

(The answer is D.)

Home economics. Students who have done some cooking or sewing, those who have engaged in relevant activities as a part-time job (for example, baby-sitting), and those who have taken home economics courses should have an advantage on these items.

A sample item follows:

Item 24. **In a recipe calling for one cup of butter, you should use**

    A. one pound.
    B. two pounds.
    C. a half-pound.
    D. a quarter-pound
    E. one-eighth pound.

(The answer is C.)

Law. These items primarily measure "general information," so that a good score on this scale is not necessarily indicative of interest in law. Nevertheless it seems probable that a student whose score in this area is relatively low is not likely to have enough interest in law to make it an advisable career for him.

Here are two sample items:

Item 25. **What kind of degree do most lawyers have from law school?**

    A. B.A.
    B. B.S.
    C. Ph.D.
    D. LL.D.
    E. LL.B.

(The answer is E.)

Item 26. **A coroner's chief function is to investigate**

    A. mysterious deaths.
    B. burglaries.
    C. counterfeiting rings.
    D. kidnapping cases.
    E. accusations of bribery.

(The answer is A.)

Health. Among the areas sampled are knowledge of physiology, nutrition, first aid, common ailments, physicians' instruments, and training requirements for medical and nursing careers.

Here is a sample item:

Item 27. **A deficiency disease is a disease caused by**

    A. a virus.
    B. improper diet.
    C. not getting inoculated.
    D. defective glands.
    E. poor heredity.

(The answer is B.)

Architecture. Those who have read books and articles about architecture and students whose interest has manifested itself in other ways — for instance, through conscious observation of the architecture around them — should do well on these items.

Farming. These items are intended to give some representation to the information that children who grow up on farms or ranches are likely to acquire. The items might give some advantage to those who have an interest in rural life.

Theater. These items should indicate an interest in the theater. (It is somewhat doubtful, however, that it is possible to get much differentiation between those who are interested in the stage as a career and those who merely are interested spectators.) Most of the items deal with theater terms (for example, greasepaint, footlights).

Here is a sample item:

Item 28. **An ingénue role in a play usually calls for**

        A. exceptional acting ability.
        B. great beauty.
        C. youthfulness.
        D. a sophisticated manner.
        E. skill as a comedian.

(The answer is C.)

Photography. These items should test information that is acquired principally through photography as a hobby, and also, to a certain extent, information picked up through reading about photography, attending exhibits, and manifesting interest in other ways.

6

We now come to a discussion of three scales dealing with a student's acquisition of facts about the world of technology. Three areas are under consideration — mechanical, electrical and electronic, and aeronautic and space information. The test items for all three were dispersed throughout the Information Test.

Mechanical Information. The assumption underlying this scale is that anyone who has both aptitude for mechanical work and interest in it will probably manage in one way or another to acquire considerable information about it. It is assumed that he would be likely to acquire such information whether or not the high school he attended offered formal instruction in mechanical subjects.

Among the first standardized tests of mechanical information were the early trade tests developed for use in the Army during World War I. In the early tests of mechanical information, unlike the more recent ones, no distinction was made between mechanical information (tools, materials, mechanics, carpentry, cabinet making, painting, printing, etc.) and electrical information. In current practice, electrical and electronic information are often covered in a separate test since individuals who do well in mechanical information tests are not necessarily well informed in electricity and electronics, and vice versa. Contemporary tests of mechanical information have proved useful for predicting success as an aircraft mechanic, auto mechanic, radio repairman, radar repairman, machinist, sheet metal worker, or welder. In World War II, the Army, Navy, and Air Force made extensive use of mechanical information tests with considerable success. Frequently mechanical information items are pictorial rather than verbal; and if verbal items are used, an effort is usually made to keep the wording simple.

The TALENT mechanical information items are of the verbal, rather than pictorial type. Each item falls into one of two categories: (1) information about tools, carpentry, and other kinds of construction, or (2) information about motors and other kinds of mechanisms. The items are about equally divided between the two categories. However, this is not important except as a way of insuring breadth of coverage, since students who do well on one type of item tend to do well on the other.

The test taps a wide range of mechanical information — about automobiles, common machines, tools. The emphasis is on information acquired through direct experience with tools and motors. The wide variety of information covered tends to equalize the opportunities of boys in urban and rural environments to score well and helps to make the scores comparable.

A sample item follows:

Item 29. **Which of these tools is best for rough-shaping wood?**

    A. Rasp
    B. Plane
    C. Level
    D. Awl
    E. File

(The answer is A.)

In interpreting scores on this test, past mechanical experience or formal training in mechanics should, of course, be considered. Certainly, too, the sex of the individual should be borne in mind in interpreting a score, since pronounced sex differences are usually found in scores on mechanical information. In general, those who score well on these items will tend to do well in training for a wide variety of mechanical occupations — for instance, machinist, artillery mechanic, sheet metal worker, foundryman, aircraft mechanic, and auto mechanic.

Electrical and Electronic Information. This scale is intended to serve as a predictor of success in such jobs as electrician, electronic technician, or radio and television repairman.

Extensive use of electrical and electronic information tests as predictors of job success dates back to about World War II. At that time, the military services found that tests of electrical and electronic information were useful in identifying persons who would make good electricians or electronic technicians (though not necessarily good mechanics). This sort of test was therefore used extensively and successfully in assigning military personnel to specific training programs. Ever since then it has been realized that the occupational fields represented by mechanical jobs and electrical jobs are functionally different. Civilian versions of electrical and electronic information tests for use in selection and counseling were not developed until recently. Such tests have proved useful in predicting success in numerous jobs, including electrician, electronic technician, radio repairman, and radar repairman.

Most of the TALENT electricity and electronics items are of the verbal type, although a few involve diagrams. The items stress information acquirable through direct experience in the construction and maintenance of electrical and electronic equipment. Thus, examinees who have worked on radios, hi-fi sets, or other electronic equipment, for instance, would have an advantage. It is inevitable that some of the items could also be answered on the basis of information acquired in formal courses in physics and to a lesser extent in chemistry. However, items that can be answered on this basis even by persons who have not had much direct experience with electrical or electronic equipment were kept to a minimum.

Scores on this scale are considerably affected by past experience in the area, but since a broad range of content is covered, the average high school student will probably have had an opportunity to acquire a fair amount of the information tested if he is at all interested in the area and has any aptitude for it.

In other words, those who get good scores are likely to have both interest in the field and aptitude for it. They could probably complete successfully any training course in the area. A low score does not indicate that a youngster lacks the ability to learn this kind of material if he is exposed to it. However, if he has not been exposed by age 16 or 18, the chances for success in electronics or electrical training programs would be substantially lowered.

Aeronautics and Space Information. This scale is intended to help identify students whose interests and aptitudes suggest they would be successful pilots.

As has already been indicated, among the discoveries made by the Aviation Psychology Research Program during World War II was the fact that one of the tests that made an important contribution to the prediction of success in pilot training was an information test heavily loaded with questions about aeronautics and related topics. Hence, the Information Test included some items on such topics as flying procedures, navigation, jet aircraft, and space exploration.

7

Scientific Attitude Scale. These items provide a subscore which should be indicative of how the individual views the world — whether he views it as a place where there are logical cause-and-effect relationships, or whether he regards it as a place where consequences are illogical and arbitrary. In the latter category fall the modern-day equivalents of the primitive beliefs that have been called "sympathetic magic." Also in the category of illogical and arbitrary consequences are the premises of palmistry, astrology, and numerology.

Each item consists of a description of a phenomenon or an occurrence. Five explanations are presented, and the task is to select the "best" one. Only one of the five explanations is reasonable and logical. Of the other four, some involve common superstitions, magic, concepts incompatible with the scientific viewpoint, or belief in the occult. Selection of other distractors, however, may primarily imply muddled thinking on the part of the examinee. (An example of the latter kind of distractor would be Option C in Sample Item 30, below.)

None of the items requires special information in science or mathematics. Whenever such information is needed to answer the question, it is presented in the item itself. For instance, in Sample Item 31 below, the odds on ten coins falling "heads up" are stated, in round numbers, in the item.

Here are two sample items:

> *Item 30.* Jim Wilson has entered many golf tournaments but has never won one. He usually does very well until the finals. But in the finals when the score is close, he tends to make a few wild shots, which result in his defeat. The best explanation of Wilson's failure to win a tournament is that
>
> A. he is just naturally unlucky.
> B. he "goes to pieces" under pressure.
> C. he hasn't practiced.
> D. he doesn't really care whether he wins.
> E. his opponents are just naturally lucky.

(The answer is B.)

> *Item 31.* Professor Rogers wished to find out whether any of the 950 students in Central High School could demonstrate the power of "mind over matter." When ten pennies are tossed, the chances that all ten of them will fall "heads up" are about one in a thousand. Rogers had each student in turn toss ten pennies. He instructed them to try, by thinking very hard about it, to make all ten pennies fall "heads up." But when one of the boys, Joe Thompson, tossed the coins they all fell "tails up." What does this suggest about Joe?
>
> A. Joe was purposely trying to get all tails.
> B. Joe became confused.
> C. Joe didn't have faith in the power of mind over matter.
> D. Joe is unlucky.
> E. Nothing.

(The answer is E.)

The Scientific Attitude scale is strictly experimental. We hope it will prove helpful in assessing scientific aptitude.

6 The Tests: Their History and Content—2

Our description of the tests continues. Here we deal with tests for memory for sentences, memory for words, and disguised words. We next describe the purpose and content for a group of tests of ability to use and comprehend the English language. Following that, we give an account of the tests dealing with creativity, mechanical reasoning, visualization, mathematical reasoning, and arithmetic computation. Finally, tests of table reading, clerical checking, and object inspection are described.

This chapter also discusses our preferences test and tells why we asked each student to write two themes — on "What High School Means to Me" and "My Views of an Ideal Occupation."

The probing for patterns of aptitude and ability continued by means of tests which sought more than a student's fact-absorbing capacities.

Previous research had indicated that human ability depends heavily on memory (probably more than one kind), language and mathematical skills, and ability to visualize movement in two or three dimensions. But perhaps central in the aptitude pattern are reasoning ability and creativity.

Therefore, in addition to testing knowledge of facts by using the Information Test we tested for the wide range of abilities suggested above. The nature and background of the tests used for these purposes are described below.

MEMORY FOR SENTENCES

There are several different aspects of memory. Which of the various aspects of memory does the TALENT Memory for Sentences Test include?

First, we believe it measures recall rather than recognition. Some researchers have said it is impossible to measure recall with an objective test — that all that can be done is to measure recognition. We disagree, and offer the Memory for Sentences Test as evidence. Next, our test measures materials which the student deliberately tries to memorize — that is, the test does not measure incidental memory. Furthermore, what it measures is something more than immediate memory, since two other tests intervened between the study period and the test period. Finally, the test was designed to measure memory for material which is underlearned, rather than overlearned. This material is verbal, consisting of sentences.

We mention the kind of memory measured by this test because it is easy (and risky) for test users to overgeneralize from the title of a test and to infer, for instance, that because a test has the word "memory" in its title it will indicate how well someone can do in all kinds of memory tasks. This is not so. There are several specific kinds of memory, and the results derived from a test of one kind should be applied to other kinds only with great caution.

This test is experimental in nature. Numerous tests of ability to memorize materials have been developed in the past, but as far as we know, the type of item used in the TALENT Memory for Sentences Test has not been used before in precisely the same form. This item type is a multiple-choice version of a kind of completion test that had been developed to measure essentially the same thing. This earlier test, developed at the Educational Testing Service, consists of a study period in which a number of sentences are to be memorized, followed by a testing period in which some or all of the same sentences are presented in a different order, with one word missing from each. The task is to fill in the missing word.

The TALENT test for memory for sentences consists of 40 short sentences. The students were given six minutes to memorize them. The test items consist of some of these sentences, in a different order, with one word omitted from each sentence. The task is to recall the missing word and identify its second letter, which is one of five options. Each option consists of only one letter, instead of an entire word, in order to test the ability to *recall* the missing word, rather than merely the ability to recognize the word when it is presented. The second letter is used instead of the first in order to minimize the extent to which the letter itself will help the person recall the missing word if he has forgotten it.

Those who do well on this kind of memory test are probably likely to do well in types of school work that call for rote learning of verbal materials, and they will also probably make good initial progress in training programs where a great deal of nomenclature or many facts are to be learned.

The following sentence might have been used as one of the 40 to be memorized:

"Mary tried to catch the four o'clock bus."

If that sentence had been used, the following could have been one of the test items:

> *Item 32.* Mary _____ to catch the four o'clock bus.
>
> A. __a _____
> E. __e _____
> I. __i _____
> R. __r _____
> U. __u _____

(The answer is r — the second letter of "tried.")

Note that many other words could be used to fill this space just as well, such as "wanted," "decided," "liked," or "hurried." However, the word in the sentence was "tried."

MEMORY FOR WORDS

The purpose of this test is to measure another kind of rote memory — the ability to memorize "foreign" words corresponding to common English words. This ability is directly relevant to learning a foreign language, and presumably related to ability to learn many other kinds of material.

Various kinds of "paired associates" tests have been used for a long time in psychological research on the nature of memory. A "paired associates" test is a test in which a set of pairs of symbols is studied for a fixed period, to associate each symbol with the one paired with it. The symbols may be numbers, diagrams, pictures, persons' names, real words, or nonsense syllables.

As early as World War I, paired associates were used to measure code learning ability. More recently, Carroll and Sapon[1] developed a "Paired Associates" Test (Test 5 in the Psi-Lambda Foreign Language Aptitude Battery) predicting ability to learn foreign languages. This test has been shown to be useful for its intended purpose. Carroll[2] found, for instance, that his "Paired Associates" Test measured a factor he designated as "associative memory" and, to a somewhat lesser extent, a factor he called "linguistic interest," both of which were related to course grades in an intensive Air Force "trial course" in Mandarin Chinese.

The TALENT Memory for Words Test is modeled directly on Test 5 (Paired Associates) of the Psi-Lambda Foreign Language Aptitude Battery.

In this test the student is given two minutes to study 24 common English words and their alleged equivalents in a totally unfamiliar language. To insure that the language would be unfamiliar to all, a language named *Vlaznoor* was invented especially for use in the TALENT test. The two-minute study period is followed by a two-minute practice period in which the students practice recall, using a list of the Vlaznoor words. Ability to select the English equivalent of a given foreign (Vlaznoor) word from among five options is then tested. Each Vlaznoor word is a separate item and is presented in a different order from that used in the learning and practice materials. Almost all options are English words used in the vocabulary studied, although an occasional English word not in the vocabulary studied may be used as a distractor — for example, "in," when "on" is the right answer.

[1] Carroll, J. B., & Sapon, S. M., *Psi-Lambda Foreign Language Aptitude Battery.* New York: Psychological Corp., 1955.

[2] Carroll, J. B., "The Factor Analysis of Two Foreign Language Aptitude Batteries." *J. Genet. Psychol.*, 1958, 59, 3–19.

The foreign words are sharply different from each other. Words that differ in only one letter (for example, DRINVO and DRANVO) are not used. Each of the foreign words is a pronounceable combination of vowels and consonants (for example, KAJELB), not an unpronounceable jumble of consonants (for example, BTFLSPKT).

A sample of the type of vocabulary used is shown below:

Foreign	English
KAJELB	walk
DRINVO	potato
HOL	ear
TAHNE	pretty
FALG	shoe

The following is a sample test item:

Item 33. **DRINVO**

    A. ear
    B. pretty
    C. shoe
    D. potato
    E. walk

(The answer is D.)

This test differs from the Memory for Sentences Test in several major respects:

The Memory for Words Test, unlike the Memory for Sentences Test, measures the recognition type of memory, not the recall type. It measures immediate memory. No other tests intervene between the study period and the test period. The material to be learned is less meaningful than that of the Memory for Sentences Test, since half of each pair of terms to be associated is an arbitrary verbal symbol.

There is considerable evidence that the ability measured by the Memory for Words Test is useful in learning a foreign language. There is also good evidence that the test would be a useful predictor of ability to learn many kinds of code. (The task imposed by the test is a form of code learning.) It is obvious that rote memory is also useful in many other kinds of jobs.

DISGUISED WORDS

This test is designed to measure what has been termed "phonetic-orthographic ability — the ability to form connections between letters and sounds."[3]

A test in which the task was to decipher words, spelled in a partially phonetic and very much abbreviated form, was used about 20 years ago as part of the Turse Shorthand Aptitude Test.[4] This test was demonstrated to be useful for its purpose of predicting ability to learn shorthand.

The task used in the Turse Shorthand Aptitude Test was adopted, in slightly more complex form, for the Spelling Clues Test (Test 3) of the Psi-Lambda Foreign Language Aptitude Battery. In this version, the task was to figure out what word was represented by the odd combination of letters and then to demonstrate that one had translated correctly by picking the correct synonym from among five choices. Carroll obtained evidence that his Spelling Clues Test was useful as a predictor of foreign language learning ability.

The TALENT Disguised Words Test uses the same type of item as the Spelling Clues Test, with the difference that we made a systematic effort to keep the vocabulary level low by limiting the words "spelled" to approximately the first 5,000 in the "Teacher's Word Book of 30,000 Words,"[5] which shows the order of frequency with which words are used in written English. We imposed this restriction to reduce to a minimum the extent to which the test measures vocabulary, since our battery already included a separate vocabulary scale in the Information Test.

The directions for the test read as follows:

"Each item begins with a word which is disguised by spelling it in a very peculiar way. However, it is spelled somewhat as it is

[3] Ibid.

[4] Turse, P. L., *Turse Shorthand Aptitude Test.* Yonkers-on-Hudson: World Book Co., 1937–40.

[5] Thorndike, E. L. and Lorge, I., *The Teacher's Word Book of 30,000 Words.* New York: Teachers College, Columbia University, 1944. (The words used were limited to those designated AA, A, or 14–49 in the G column of the word list.)

pronounced. The disguised word is followed by five real words or phrases. . . . Show that you recognize the disguised word by selecting the choice that means most nearly the same thing. . . ."

Two sample items follow:

Item 34. **DLA**

> A. sadly
> B. postpone
> C. bluntly
> D. hand out
> E. every day

(The answer is B, since the disguised word is *delay*.)

Item 35. **DSKRIJD**

> A. depressed
> B. described
> C. thrown away
> D. ruined
> E. accused

(The answer is A, since the disguised word is *discouraged*.)

As was pointed out, the items are not intended to measure vocabulary directly, except to a very limited degree. Nor are they intended to measure spelling ability. (This, too, is measured directly by another test in the battery.)

What the test measures is the ability to puzzle out, from context and appearances, the meaning of a word which is vaguely reminiscent of a familiar English word. To put it another way, what is measured, to a considerable extent, is ability to draw inferences of a type that would be drawn in learning to read a foreign language. The ability measured is probably also useful in learning shorthand.

ENGLISH

The purpose of this test is to measure ability to express oneself adequately in English. It has five separately scored parts:

1. Spelling
2. Capitalization
3. Punctuation
4. English Usage
5. Effective Expression

It also yields a total score, which indicates overall achievement in various aspects of English expression measurable by objective test items.

The test is primarily concerned with written English, but presumably some generalization to spoken English on the basis of the English Usage and Effective Expression subscores is justifiable.

Each of the five parts of the test is discussed in turn.

1. Spelling. Each item consists of four words, of which one may be misspelled. The task is to determine which one of the four, if any, is misspelled.

Below are two sample items:

Item 36.

    A. excellent
    B. exercise
    C. exstract
    D. extreme
    E. None of the above

Item 37.

    A. affection
    B. complexion
    C. electrician
    D. permission
    E. None of the above

(The answers to these two items are C and E, respectively.)

The test measures ability to spell reasonably common words — words that have probably been encountered at least once by almost all of the students. The words are not necessarily ones that students can define — it is possible for good spellers to know how to spell words they do not understand. To insure that the vocabulary would not be too difficult, the words tested were limited to the 10,000 used most frequently in written English, according to the Thorndike-Lorge word list.

Except in the case of such activities as proofreading and editing, the ability to spell correctly when writing is generally more important than the ability to recognize spelling errors when one is not writing. Although what is measured *directly* by the test is ability to recognize spelling errors when presented with the visual stimulus, the actual ability to spell a word correctly when writing it is probably tapped indirectly. No effort is made to measure the ability to spell orally.

A spelling test was included in the battery for two reasons. First, the kind of achievement measured by this test is inherently important. The ability to spell adequately is necessary in order to be able to write acceptable English. This ability is essential for many types of jobs. The ability to recognize spelling errors is also directly necessary to many job activities.

The second reason for including spelling in the battery was that its correlation with many other aptitude tests is quite low; therefore it could be expected to contribute a unique component. Relatively little is known about what spelling ability actually consists of — to what extent it depends on visual memory, visual perception, or auditory-visual association. But there is evidence that its inclusion in a battery contributes significantly to the battery's validity for a number of purposes.

2. *Capitalization.* This test, which measures mastery of the rules of capitalization, consists of a passage printed entirely in lower case letters. The task is to determine which of the words with numbers under them should start with a capital letter.

Below is a sample passage with 36 items:

```
george  hathaway  spent  last  november  in  paris  with  his
38      39                40     41              42        43
brother  henry  and  their  young  cousin,  louis  beauregard;
44       45     46    47     48       49     50
they  stayed  in  rather  a  large  hotel  overlooking  the  seine
51            52     53 54     55     56                57  58
river.  in  december  they  all  went  to  england  (to  london,  i
59      60 61               62          63           64 65       66
```

believe), where they spent christmas with dr. and mrs.
      67   68   69   70   71   72

hathaway.
73

(Answers: The words to be capitalized are Nos. 38, 39, 41, 42, 45, 49, 50, 58, 59, 60, 61, 63, 65, 66, 70, 71, 72, 73.)

3. Punctuation. The Punctuation subtest has two parts — Section *a* (Punctuation Marks) and Section *b* (Sentence Structure).

In Section *a*, each item consists of a sentence, part of which is printed without punctuation. This part of the sentence is then presented punctuated in several alternative ways. The task is to determine which is correct.

A sample item follows:

   Item 74. **How blue the sky has turned**

        A. sky has turned.
        B. sky has turned!
        C. sky has turned?
        D. sky, has turned.
        E. sky; has turned.

   (The answer is B.)

The purpose of Section *a* is to test knowledge of the appropriate use of standard punctuation marks. While the pupil is required to differentiate between correct and incorrect punctuation, he is not required to determine which of two or more acceptable manners of punctuation is preferable. For instance, no effort is made to test whether the student recognizes cases where although a period is grammatically correct, a semicolon would be preferable; nor is any effort made to test whether the student has the same preference as the item writer in cases where either commas, dashes, or parentheses are technically acceptable.

In Section *b*, each item consists of either a fragment of a sentence, a complete sentence, or two or more sentences run together. The task is to determine which it is. The instructions are to mark the answer sheet as follows:

Mark "0" if it is part of a sentence.
Mark "1" if it is one complete sentence.
Mark "2" if it is two or more sentences run together.

Four sample items follow:

> *Item 75.* **A course of study including English, French, algebra, American history, and chemistry.**

> *Item 76.* **The football team having tied one game and won all the rest.**

> *Item 77.* **It's late, let's get started.**

> *Item 78.* **Do you know how?**

(The answers are 0, 0, 2, and 1, respectively.)

4. English Usage. Each item consists of a sentence with a word or group of words missing, the missing section being represented by a blank. The task is to determine which of several (three to five) choices fits best in the blank. The instructions specify that if two choices are correct, the better one is to be selected.

Here are two sample items:

> *Item 79.* **Bob _____ arrange it.**
>
> > A. might could
> > B. might be able to
> > C. could maybe
> > D. maybe could
> > E. would maybe be able to

(The answer is B.)

> *Item 80.* **Ed and _____ planning to go.**
>
> > A. myself was
> > B. me was
> > C. I was
> > D. myself were
> > E. I were

(The answer is E.)

The items measure knowledge of correct English usage and the ability to express a given idea in the most desirable way. The student is required to decide which of several options provides the best (grammatically correct, clearest, least ambiguous, least awkward) way of expressing an idea.

5. *Effective Expression.* Each item consists of three, four, or five sentences, each expressing the same idea, but only one of them expressing it well. The student is to select which of the sentences expresses the idea best. He is given no hint as to what criteria to use in making his decision.

A sample item follows:

Item 81.

A. Things such as this helped our forefathers push back the wilderness and create the richest nation in the world.
B. Our forefathers created the richest nation in the world, helped by things like this to push back the wilderness.
C. Things such as this helped our forefathers in their pushing back of the wilderness and in their creation of the richest nation in the world.
D. To create the richest nation in the world, our forefathers, being helped by things like this, pushed back the wilderness.

(The answer is A.)

These items are used to measure recognition of whether an idea has been expressed clearly, concisely, and smoothly. The student is not required to determine whether the preferred sentence represents the *best possible* way of expressing the idea. He need only choose among the sentences given.

Word Functions in Sentences

This test is intended to measure the student's sensitivity to grammatical structure, whether or not he has had instruction in the rules of grammar.

This type of test was originated a few years ago by John B. Carroll, who designed it as a measure of foreign language aptitude and incorporated it in his Psi-Lambda Foreign Language Aptitude Battery[6] as Test 4 (Words in Sentences). It has proved to have excellent validity as a predictor of foreign language learning ability.

The TALENT Word Functions in Sentences Test uses the same type of item as the Words in Sentences Test (Test 4 of the Carroll-Sapon Psi-Lambda Battery) mentioned above. Each item consists of a "key sentence," followed by one or more other sentences. One word or phrase in the key sentence is printed in capital letters. The task is to determine which of five underlined words or phrases in the following sentence or sentences performs the same function in its sentence as the capitalized word or phrase performs in *its* sentence.

Three sample items follow:

Item 82. **They walked GAILY down the street.**

The <u>newly</u> arrived couple <u>used</u> up their <u>money</u> <u>too</u> <u>fast</u>.
     A   B   C   D E

Item 83. **Judy, HAVING an optimistic nature, expected things to turn out well.**

<u>Driving</u> a car requires a license.
  A

The weather <u>having</u> finally cleared up, Mrs. Rogers
              B
was able to work in her garden.

Helen, busily <u>planning</u> her afternoon, wasn't <u>watching</u>
           C   D
where she was <u>going.</u>
        E

Item 84. **This is the WAY to do it.**

I do it a different <u>way.</u>
        A
I use a different <u>method.</u>
        B

[6] Op. cit.

The way to do it is like this.
    C

That's the wrong method.
       D

There are many ways of doing it.
      E

(The answers to these three items are E, C, and D, respectively.)

This test was deliberately made very difficult, since there is reason to believe a hard test would predict ability to learn foreign languages better than an easier one.

Although formal training in grammar and study of foreign languages (particularly of highly inflected ones, such as Latin) are probably of some help on this test, the fact that the terminology of grammar is not used reduces the effects of formal training to a minimum. To perform well on this test, one must understand the structure of a sentence and recognize the function of each word or phrase in the sentence. This ability is probably related to the ability to learn the grammar and characteristic sentence structure of a foreign language — particularly one in which word order is typically different from that of English. It is probably also related to the ability to learn the formal rules of English grammar.

Although a relationship has been found between scores on this type of test and the ability to learn a foreign language, a high score on the test does not guarantee success in mastering a foreign language; this test measures only one aspect of that complex ability. But considered in conjunction with other relevant tests, the Word Functions in Sentences Test should prove useful as a predictor.

READING COMPREHENSION

The purpose of the test is to measure ability to comprehend written materials.

The most common of the numerous types of standardized reading tests used over the last 40 years consists of passages to be read, with each passage followed by several multiple-choice questions testing comprehension. This is the type that was chosen for the TALENT battery. In answering the questions the student is permitted to refer back to the passage as often as he likes.

Like its predecessors, the TALENT test includes passages covering a wide range of topics. Some deal with social studies, some with natural science, and some with literary content. Poetry as well as prose is included.

A poem and some sample items based on it follow:

(1) Loveliest of trees, the cherry now
(2) Is hung with bloom along the bough
(3) And stands about the woodland ride
(4) Wearing white for Eastertide.

(5) Now, of my threescore years and ten,
(6) Twenty will not come again,
(7) And take from seventy springs a score,
(8) It only leaves me fifty more.

(9) And since to look at things in bloom
(10) Fifty springs are little room,
(11) About the woodlands I will go
(12) To see the cherry hung with snow.[7]

Item 85. What does the word "ride" probably mean, as used in line 3?

    A. Auto ride
    B. Tree
    C. Horseback ride
    D. Flowers
    E. Road

[7] "Loveliest of Trees," from "A Shropshire Lad" — Authorized Edition, from COMPLETE POEMS by A. E. Housman. Copyright © 1959 by Holt, Rinehart and Winston, Inc. Reprinted in the United States and its possessions by permission of Holt, Rinehart and Winston, Inc., New York, New York. Reprinted outside the U.S. and its dependencies by permission of The Society of Authors, literary representatives of the estate of the late A. E. Housman and Messrs. Jonathan Cape, Ltd., publishers of A. E. Housman's COLLECTED POEMS.

Item 86. **What season is it, in the poem?**

    A. Winter
    B. Spring
    C. Summer
    D. Fall
    E. There is no way of telling.

Item 87. **The poet indicates, a little ruefully, that his life**

    A. will pass too quickly.
    B. will probably end very soon.
    C. has been unhappy.
    D. has been devoid of beauty.
    E. has been uneventful.

Item 88. **How old does the poet say he is?**

    A. 20
    B. 30
    C. 40
    D. 50
    E. 70

Item 89. **When the poet says he "will go" (line 11), he probably means he will go**

    A. on foot.
    B. by boat.
    C. by automobile.
    D. by horse-drawn sleigh.
    E. on snowshoes or skis.

(The answers are E, B, A, A, and A, respectively.)

It is important to note that this test measures ability to read with comprehension, rather than mere ability to recognize the printed word without understanding the fact, idea, or concept expressed.

Reading comprehension skills have been classified into the following nine categories:

"1. Knowledge of word meanings.
2. Ability to select the appropriate meaning for a word or phrase in the light of its particular contextual setting.
3. Ability to follow the organization of a passage and to identify antecedents and references in it.

4. Ability to select the main thought of a passage.
5. Ability to answer questions that are specifically answered in a passage.
6. Ability to answer questions that are answered in a passage but not in the words in which the question is asked.
7. Ability to draw inferences from a passage about its contents.
8. Ability to recognize the literary devices used in a passage to determine its tone and mood.
9. Ability to determine a writer's purpose, intent, and point of view — i.e., to draw inferences about a writer."[8]

Of these nine categories, all but the first is covered directly by items in this test. Knowledge of word meanings is measured in the Information Test vocabulary scale and therefore is not measured directly in the Reading Comprehension Test. To a certain extent, however, knowledge of word meanings will affect Reading Comprehension scores, since the vocabulary of the passages and questions must be reasonably well understood if the items are to be answered correctly. However, extremely difficult vocabulary has been avoided. In general, the vocabulary is within the first 15,000 words on the Thorndike-Lorge List.[9] The primary exceptions to this limitation would be words whose meaning is explained in the passage and words whose meaning can be inferred reasonably well from the context.

The ability measured by this test is a good predictor of school success in an academic or liberal arts curriculum.

CREATIVITY

The purpose of this test is to measure the ability to find ingenious solutions to practical problems. There is some evidence that this ability is related to many kinds of creativity.

Many attempts have been made to measure creativity or ingenuity. Perhaps the most comprehensive effort in recent years has been that of Guilford,[10] who studied the interrelations of

[8] Davis, F. B., "Fundamental Factors of Comprehension in Reading," *Psychometrika*, 1944, 9, 185–197.
[9] Op. cit.
[10] Guilford, J. P., "The Structure of Intellect," *Psych. Bull.*, 1953, 267–293.

many tests of fluency, imagination, and originality. A recent development is the new item type designed by Flanagan to measure ingenuity and inventive skill — the ability to devise ingenious procedures, equipment, or presentations. He developed a new response format which avoids suggesting the correct responses to the problems as presented. The examinee is given the problem and a few clues and is required to devise an ingenious solution. This is the type of item used in the Ingenuity Test of the Flanagan Aptitude Classification Tests (FACT Battery).[11]

The TALENT Creativity Test is modeled on the FACT Ingenuity Test described above. Each item consists of a complex problem similar to one that might be encountered in life. The student is required to think of a clever or ingenious solution. The choices are given in terms of the first and last letters of possible right answers. This is to insure that the student really develops the solution, instead of just selecting it from among five choices.

Two sample items are given below:

Item 90. The sanding and smoothing of knobs and other small round wooden objects is a problem because flat sheets of sandpaper do not fit the knobs. The sandpaper buckles and tends to wrinkle. One solution is to cut several

A. e _ _ _ _ _ _ n d _ _ _ s in the sandpaper.
B. h _ _ _ _ _ _ l t _ _ _ s in the sandpaper.
C. p _ _ _ _ _ _ l s _ _ _ s in the sandpaper.
D. t _ _ _ _ _ _ n w _ _ _ s in the sandpaper.
E. m _ _ _ _ _ _ h b _ _ _ s in the sandpaper.

(The answer is C, since "parallel slits" is the solution.)

Item 91. Attic and cellar stairways and stepladders are often causes of household accidents. One method for preventing slipping and falling on wooden stairs or steps is to apply a coat of varnish to each step, and while

[11] Flanagan, J. C., Flanagan Aptitude Classification Tests. Chicago: Science Research Associates, 1957.

the varnish is still slightly sticky, apply a small amount of

A. d _ _ n to each step.
B. s _ _ d to each step.
C. r _ _ g to each step.
D. g _ _ n to each step.
E. r _ _ t to each step.

(The answer is B, since "sand" is the solution.)

The items do not require detailed knowledge of specialized fields. They *are* intended to provide a measure of something beyond general knowledge, vocabulary, and deductive reasoning ability. There is evidence that they do. As would be expected from an examination of the items, the Creativity Test measures to some extent the ability measured by various kinds of reasoning tests, including mechanical reasoning. However, it has an appreciable amount of "unique reliable variance"; in other words, part of what it measures is an ability not covered by any other kinds of paper-and-pencil tests that have been tried out in conjunction with it.

High scores on this test should be interpreted as indicating inventiveness or creative ingenuity.

MECHANICAL REASONING

The purpose of this test is to measure ability to visualize the effects of everyday physical forces and principles (for example, gravitation, pressure, equilibrium) and the operation of basic kinds of mechanisms (for example, gears, pulleys, wheels, springs, levers). Tests of this sort have sometimes been called measures of "barnyard physics." The ability measured is related to mechanical aptitude.

As early as World War I, mechanical ability was recognized as a type of testable ability separate from general intelligence. Later, various combinations of manipulative, pictorial, and verbal items were used to test mechanical ability. It was not until much later that psychologists recognized that the different types of "mechanical" items were really measuring somewhat different mental factors. In 1940 the Bennett Mechanical Comprehension Test[12] was developed.

By the end of World War II the broad area of mechanical ability had been resolved into such commonly used tests as mechanical information, electrical information, tool usage, spatial visualization, eye-hand coordination, and pictorial mechanical reasoning. The latter, in the form employed by Bennett, has been the most widely used. However, many comprehensive aptitude test batteries employ most or all of these types of tests. Despite the relatively high correlation between scores on the various types, all have proven to yield some unique contribution toward predicting success in mechanical occupations. The kind of ability measured by a mechanical reasoning test of the pictorial type is only one of the abilities needed for success in mechanical occupations.

There is a wealth of evidence supporting the validity of mechanical reasoning tests for a variety of occupations, such as airplane pilot, auto mechanic, machinist, welder, aircraft mechanic, sheet metal worker, and tool and die maker. Such tests have been widely used by the Armed Forces for initial selection and for assignment to training. In the extensive validation studies conducted in the Armed Forces, tests of this sort have usually been found to correlate substantially with measures of success in mechanical training courses. These results are confirmed by similar studies in industry.

The TALENT Mechanical Reasoning Test uses about the same type of items used in Bennett's Mechanical Comprehension Tests. Each item consists of a drawing, with a multiple choice question on how the objects pictured behave.

Getting a good score on this test calls for visualization, reasoning, and "intuitive" understanding based on past observation of common mechanical forces at work. Every item can be answered without training in physics, and without experience in woodworking or other crafts, or in working with motors. Nor is knowledge of tools or of electricity measured. Nevertheless, the student's past training and experience should be borne in mind in interpreting the results. A course in physics may make many of the items easier. The fact that girls, on the average,

[12] Bennett, G. K., *Tests of Mechanical Comprehension.* New York: Psychological Corp., 1940.

score considerably lower than boys is consistent with the hypothesis that training, experience, and other environmental factors play a role in the development of mechanical reasoning. However, this does not render the test any less useful as a predictor of success in mechanical jobs.

A sample item is shown below:

> *Item 92.* When worm gear X is turned in the direction shown, in which direction, if any, does gear Y turn?

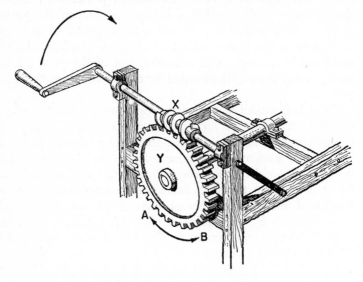

A. In direction A
B. In direction B
C. First in one direction and then in the other
D. It doesn't turn.

(The answer is A.)

VISUALIZATION IN TWO DIMENSIONS
and
VISUALIZATION IN THREE DIMENSIONS

The purpose of these two tests is to measure spatial visualization — the ability to visualize how an object, pattern, or configuration would appear when viewed from various angles in various positions.

Spatial visualization has been measured by a great many different kinds of tests — some involving visualization in two dimensions and some involving visualization in three. It was decided to measure spatial ability with two separate tests in the TALENT battery, a two-dimensional visualization test and a three-dimensional one, although it was expected that the resultant scores would be rather highly correlated. Precautions were taken in both tests to insure that what was measured would be visualization ability, not visual acuity. To reduce the role of exceptional visual acuity, all diagrams were drawn large and free of detail.

Visualization in Two Dimensions.   One kind of test measuring two-dimensional visualization is a test of the ability to distinguish between figures that have been rotated on a flat surface and figures that have been manipulated in another way — specifically, non-symmetrical figures that have been turned over to produce mirror images.

The following are the instructions that the students received for this test in the Project TALENT battery:

"Look at the drawings below:

"The first drawing is shaped like the letter L. The rest of the drawings are like the first, except that they have been turned in different directions.

"If you think of the drawing at the left above as being made out of wire and lying on a table, the positions shown in each of the other four drawings could be taken simply by turning the wire figure at the left around, without lifting it off the table.

"Now look at the next row of drawings.

"The first drawing is shaped like the letter P. But even if the rest of the drawings were turned around, they would still be backwards; you would have to lift the figure at the left off the table and flip it over to make any of the other figures.

"In this test each problem has one drawing at the left and five similar drawings to the right of it, but only one of the five drawings on the right exactly matches the drawing at the left if you turn it around. The rest of the drawings are backwards even when they are turned around.

"Now look at the sample problem below.

"Which one of the choices, when turned around, exactly matches the diagram at the left?

S1.

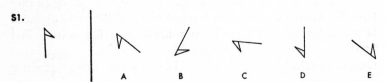

"You should have picked choice D. All of the other choices have been 'lifted off the table and flipped over' as well as turned around, and thus are backwards. For the sample problem, answer space D has been marked on your answer sheet.

"For each problem in this test, choose the one drawing which, when turned around or rotated, is exactly like the basic drawing at the left."

Here is another sample item.

Item 93.

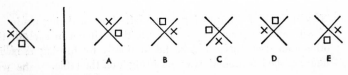

(The answer is B.)

Visualization in Three Dimensions. Among the many kinds of tests measuring three-dimensional visualization are tests measuring the ability to visualize

1) how a two-dimensional figure would look after it had been folded to make a three-dimensional figure;

2) how a three-dimensional figure would look after it had been unfolded or flattened out (sometimes called surface development);

3) the rotation of solid figures, such as cubes;

4) solid figures on the basis of top, front, and side projections;

5) hidden parts of solid structures (as in a "block-counting test," where the task might be to determine how many cubical blocks there are in an irregularly shaped structure, not all of which is visible).

Although the tasks involved in these various types of items differ widely, an analysis of their correlations indicates that most of them measure essentially the same kind of ability.

This ability is involved in many technical, mechanical, and engineering occupations such as design engineer, carpenter, mechanical draftsman, and airplane pilot. Tests of this sort are useful for selecting students who are likely to do well in shop courses. These tests are also useful in vocational situations where the individual must make a quick adaptation to the demands of certain semi-skilled jobs — especially those involving the assembly of irregularly shaped parts, machine operation, and the packing of objects of different shapes and sizes.

It was decided to make the Project TALENT Visualization in Three Dimensions Test the first of the five kinds mentioned above; that is, to design it to measure the ability to visualize what a two-dimensional figure would look like if it were folded or rolled to form a three-dimensional figure. Folds are indicated in the diagrams by dotted lines, and cuts by interior solid lines.

These are the instructions that the students received for this test:

"Each problem in this test has a drawing of a flat piece of metal at the left. At the right are shown five objects, only one of which might be made by folding the flat piece of metal along the dotted lines.

"You are to pick out the one of these five objects which shows just how the piece of flat metal will look when it is folded at the dotted lines. When it is folded, no piece of metal overlaps any other piece, or is enclosed inside the object.

"Now look at the sample item.

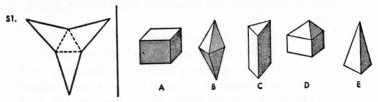

"Of the five objects shown, only E could be made from the flat piece shown at the left by folding it at each of the dotted lines. E shows how the flat piece would look after being folded. Answer space E has been marked for sample item S1 on your answer sheet.

"Remember, all folds are indicated by dotted lines; the solid lines show the cuts in the piece, and parts are not folded inside of other parts of any objects (in other words, there is no overlapping)."

Here is another sample item; this one a relatively hard one:

Item 94.

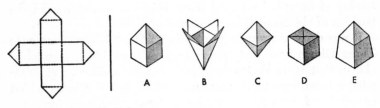

(The answer is D.)

Abstract Reasoning

This is a non-verbal test of one kind of abstract inductive reasoning ability. The problems require reasoning about diagrams, and do not include any verbal material.

Originally one of the major purposes of non-verbal reasoning tests was to measure the basic aptitude for school learning of individuals with language handicaps. Efforts along these lines were made even before World War I. It has since been found, however, that the kind of abstract reasoning ability measured by non-verbal reasoning tests is not the same thing as the kind of ability measured by verbal tests. This fact makes a test of this type more generally useful than it would be if its applicability were limited to persons with language handicaps. Many currently used scholastic aptitude tests include measures of abstract non-verbal reasoning, as do most multiple aptitude batteries.

Several different types of items measuring ability to do abstract reasoning about diagrammatic material have been widely used. Among these types are figure analogies items, figure sequences items, pattern matrices items, and figure grouping items. The first three of these item types all consist of a pattern or diagram, with one missing portion to be selected from among several options. In the fourth item type, figure grouping, the task is a little different; it is to determine what the principle is which ties several diagrams together, and on the basis of this principle to determine which pattern from among several options belongs with the group of patterns.

Sample items of each type are shown below:

Item 95. (Figure analogy item)

Item 96. (Figure sequence item)

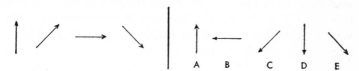

Item 97. (Pattern matrix item)

Item 98. (Figure grouping item)

(The answers are C, D, D, and C, respectively)

In these types of abstract reasoning items, the solution depends upon the ability to determine a logical relationship among elements of the pattern and to apply this relationship in order to identify an element that belongs in the pattern. The task may be to identify an element that belongs in a specified position in the pattern. This is the case for the figure analogies, figure sequences, or pattern matrices tests. Or, the task may be to identify an element that just belongs in the group but not in any specific position. This is the case in the figure grouping test.

On the basis of empirical data there seems to be relatively little clear evidence that any of the types of items discussed above is markedly superior to the others. However, a choice had to be made, and it was therefore decided to use the pattern matrices form of item in the TALENT test because it seemed to have the advantage of somewhat greater generality than the other item types. Essentially both figure analogies and figure sequences are special cases of pattern matrices. Almost any figure analogy item can be translated into the pattern matrices format, using a 2 × 2 matrix. For instance, if figure analogy item 95 were converted to the pattern matrices format, it would appear as shown in sample item 99.

Item 99.

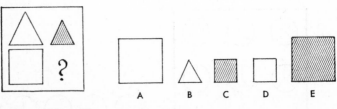

(The answer is C)

Similarly, the figure sequence type of item is readily convertible to the pattern matrices format. For instance, consider figure sequence item 96. Three pattern matrices versions of the same item are shown, as sample items 100, 101, and 102.

Item 100.

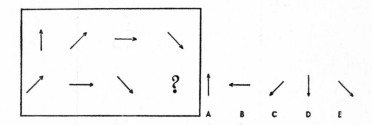

Item 101.

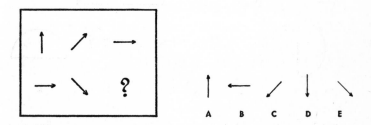

Item 102.

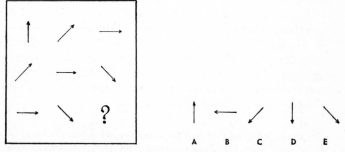

(The answer for each of these three items is D.)

These are the instructions that the students were given:

"Each item in this test consists of a set of figures arranged in a pattern, formed according to certain rules. Look at the pattern in sample item 1.

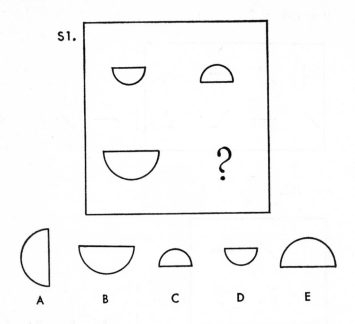

"The question mark in the lower right corner of the box shows where a figure is missing in the pattern. You are to decide which of the five figures (A, B, C, D, or E) under the pattern belongs where the question mark is. In the case of the sample item above, the figure at the left in the bottom row is larger than the one above it but otherwise the same. In the top row the figure at the right is the same as the one to the left of it except that it has been turned upside down. Following these rules, the missing figure should be larger than the one above it, and exactly the same size as the one to the left of it, but upside down. Therefore E is the answer to this problem.

"In each problem you are to decide what figure belongs where the question mark is in the pattern. To do this you have to figure out what the rule is according to which the drawings change, going from row to row, and what the rule is for the changes going from column to column. The items have different kinds of patterns and different rules by which the drawings change. Look at the next problem.

S2.

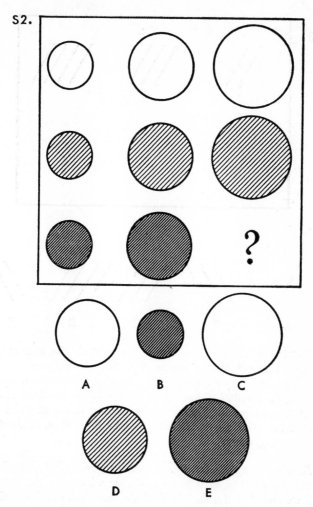

"Going from left to right, the circles get larger, and going from top to bottom they get darker. Therefore the answer has to be a circle which is the largest of the three sizes, and the darkest. Choices C and E are both the right size, but E is the only large circle with the correct shading. Thus E is the only drawing that fits in the pattern formed by the other circles. E is the answer, and therefore answer space E has been marked on the answer sheet for this item.

"Now look at another problem, which is quite different from either of the above ones.

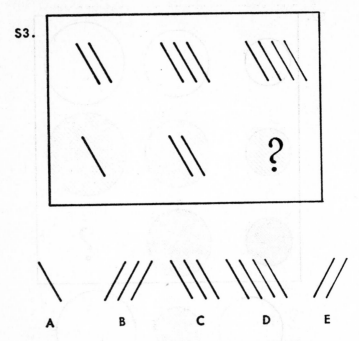

S3.

      A   B   C   D   E

"What is the missing figure here? If you study the pattern you will see that going from left to right there is one more line in each figure than in the one to the left of it. Going from top to bottom, the number of lines in any figure is one less than in the figure just above it. Therefore the missing figure should have three lines. The answer is choice C (the three lines, slanting in the proper direction).

"When you are given the signal, turn the page and start working the problems. For each problem decide what rules the pattern follows and find the answer that fits these rules and therefore 'fits in' with the rest of the pattern. Many of the patterns are based on rules that are different from the ones in the sample item."

MATHEMATICS PART I (ARITHMETIC REASONING)

This test is designed to measure the ability to do the kind of reasoning required to solve arithmetic problems.

Objective arithmetic reasoning items have frequently been used in academic aptitude tests. The chief difference between the TALENT test in arithmetic reasoning and most other tests of this ability is that in the TALENT test we made an effort to eliminate almost all computation. The aim of the TALENT test is solely to determine whether the student can do the reasoning part of a problem — not whether he will do the subsequent computation carefully enough to avoid careless errors, nor whether he knows number combinations. The intention was to measure these latter facts and abilities in the Arithmetic Computation test and to try to avoid "contaminating" the Arithmetic Reasoning test with them. Several devices were used to achieve this end. One such device was to require the student to tell how he would solve a problem but not to require him to do the necessary computation.

Two sample items are shown below:

> Item 103. **Three per cent of a certain number is 141. To find the number, you would**
>
> A. divide 141 by .03
> B. divide 141 by 3
> C. divide 141 by 300
> D. multiply 141 by .03
> E. multiply 141 by 300

(The answer is A.)

> Item 104. **Mrs. Rogers buys 6¼ pounds of apples. She gives the clerk a one-dollar bill. What single other fact is needed to find out how much change she should get?**
>
> A. Price per apple
> B. Number of apples per pound
> C. Number of ounces in a pound
> D. Price per pound of apples
> E. Weight of an average apple

(The answer is D.)

In addition, we used items which presented several facts and then asked which one was not needed in solving the problem; and items which presented several facts and then asked which one of several problems could not be solved on the basis of the facts given.

Arithmetic reasoning is perhaps the sort of test in which the relationship between aptitude and achievement can best be clarified. An arithmetic reasoning test measures *achievement* in something which has been taught, since virtually everyone in our culture today goes to school long enough to be exposed to arithmetic problems at the sixth and seventh grade level. But it also measures aptitude — the aptitude for more advanced mathematics and the aptitude for many kinds of jobs. Arithmetic reasoning tests can therefore also be thought of as aptitude tests.

MATHEMATICS PART II (INTRODUCTORY)
and
MATHEMATICS PART III (ADVANCED)

The purpose of these two subtests is to measure achievement in mathematics taught in high school (or earlier). Naturally, we have omitted from these sections any items which might have overlapped the Arithmetic Computation test and Mathematics Part I (Arithmetic Reasoning).

Tests in college preparatory mathematics, such as algebra, geometry, and trigonometry, are more appropriately regarded as measures of achievement than of aptitude. Thus, these two subtests are to be regarded primarily as achievement tests. Although there is little precedent for including such tests in a primarily predictive battery such as we have attempted to build, they should serve a useful purpose because achievement in mathematics has been found to be quite a good predictor of success in many kinds of college curricula — the applied sciences, as well as liberal arts.

The items are intended to test understanding of basic concepts and methods, rather than rote memory. Little emphasis is placed on facts and definitions since this domain is covered in the Mathematics scale of the Information Test.

In Mathematics Part II (Introductory), the emphasis is on ninth-grade elementary algebra, but other areas tested include fractions, decimals, per cents, intuitive geometry, elementary measurement formulas, and square root. Algebra is involved in over 60 per cent of the items. Computation is kept to a minimum.

Two sample items follow:

Item 105. The area of a rectangle s inches wide is three times the area of a square with a side s inches long. The length of the rectangle is

A. $\dfrac{s^2}{3}$

B. $3s$

C. $3s^2$

D. $\dfrac{s}{3}$

E. $3\sqrt{s}$

Item 106. What is the first digit of the square root of 485726? (Hint: Do *not* compute the square root.)

A. 1
B. 2
C. 4
D. 6
E. 7

(The answers are B and D, respectively.)

In Mathematics Part III (Advanced), the items sample a wide range of concepts not usually studied until Grade 10 or later. Among the areas included are plane geometry, solid geometry, algebra (quadratic equations and beyond), trigonometry, elements of analytic geometry, and introductory calculus.

Sample items follow:

Item 107. If $10^m = r^4$, the value of $\log_{10}r$ is

A. $4m$
B. m^4
C. 4^m

D. $\dfrac{m}{4}$

E. $\sqrt[4]{m}$

Item 108. If $a < b < c < e$ and $d > b$, it follows that

A. $d < c$
B. $a > d$
C. $d > a$
D. $c < d$
E. $d < e$

Item 109. A ratio which is always the same is the ratio of a circle's

    A. area to its circumference.
    B. radius to its area.
    C. circumference to π.
    D. diameter to π.
    E. radius to its circumference.

(The answers are D, C, and E, respectively.)

This subtest is intended primarily to provide a national inventory of students who have reached specified levels of achievement in mathematics. As with the other tests, norms were obtained for each grade separately. Thus, there is a suitable base for interpretation of ninth grade results, taking into consideration the fact that most of the ninth-graders will not have had formal instruction in the topics covered.

ARITHMETIC COMPUTATION

The purpose of the test is to measure speed and accuracy of computation. The test is limited to the four basic operations (addition, subtraction, multiplication, and division), and to whole numbers.

The ability measured by an aptitude test of this sort has been found important in occupations that involve quantitative work — accountant, bank teller, business manager, machinist, bookkeeper, auditor. Scores on this type of test do not have a high correlation with scores on arithmetic reasoning, or on other mathematics tests. Thus an outstandingly good score on Arithmetic Computation is not necessary in order to do well in mathematics in high school and college. It is nonetheless true that skill in arithmetic computation is helpful even in advanced mathematics, because a computational error in the early stages of a difficult problem can turn it into a nightmare; while facility in this skill leaves the mind free to concentrate on the reasoning and to proceed expeditiously to a solution.

The TALENT Arithmetic Computation Test includes operations with single-digit and multi-digit numbers. The operations tested are limited to relatively simple ones. Computation of square roots is not tested, nor is computation involving decimals, fractions, or per cents.

Sample items are shown below:

Item 110. **Add:**		A. 472
	423	B. 475
	33	C. 485
	29	D. 575
		E. 585

Item 111. **Subtract:**		A. 340
	403	B. 366
	−37	C. 376
		D. 377
		E. 476

Item 112. **Multiply:**		A. 1824
	206	B. 18024
	×94	C. 19364
		D. 19464
		E. 19564

Item 113. **Divide:**		A. 461
	3402 ÷ 6 =	B. 531
		C. 561
		D. 567
		E. 667

(The answers are C, B, C, and D, respectively.)

TABLE READING

The purpose of this test is to measure speed and accuracy of perception in a clerical task which involves obtaining information from tables.

This type of test was developed during World War II, in the Air Force Aviation Psychology Program, as a "job sample" test for selecting navigators. The test was later found to be useful in predicting success in a wide variety of occupational activities, some of them not directly concerned with table reading. Table reading tests are useful predictors for such jobs as clerk-typist, draftsman, secretary, accountant, bookkeeper, statistician, statistical clerk, shipping clerk, and navigator. Of course, the test is relevant to only one aspect of these jobs and therefore a high score on it does not guarantee success in the job, since other aptitudes and abilities are involved.

The Table Reading test consists of a table with instructions on how to use it, together with a number of multiple choice items that have to be answered by reading the table. The time allowance is very brief, to insure that no one has time to finish.

CLERICAL CHECKING

This test is designed to measure speed and accuracy of perception in a very simple clerical task involving working with pairs of names to determine whether they are identical.

Tests of this sort usually consist of pairs of names, numbers, groups of letters, or combinations; the task is to indicate whether the two elements of the pair are exactly the same or different. These tests always have a very short time limit, so that no one will have time to finish. Ordinarily a very large number of items can be compared in a very short period of time.

These tests measure one of the important aptitudes involved in clerical work. Tests of this sort have been found relevant to success not only in a wide variety of clerical jobs but also in many other jobs which are essentially non-clerical in nature but which have a substantial component requiring this type of accuracy; for instance, accounting.

A test of this type, on which the TALENT Clerical Checking Test is modeled, is an important part of the United States Employment Service's General Aptitude Test Battery.[13]

The TALENT Clerical Checking Test consists of pairs of names. The task is to compare the two names and mark S if they are exactly the same and D if they are different. Below are three sample items:

13 United States Employment Service, *USES General Aptitude Test Battery*. Washington, D.C.: The Occupational Analysis Division, United States Employment Service, 1947.

Item 114. **Joe Abernathy**   **Joe Abernethy**

Item 115. **Charles Q. Piltdown**   **Charles Q. Piltdown**

Item 116. **Mary Ann Wilsson**   **Marianne Wilsson**

(The answers are D, S, and D, respectively.)

OBJECT INSPECTION

The purpose of this test is to measure speed and accuracy of perception of form. More specifically, it is intended to measure the ability to note differences in small objects quickly and accurately when comparing them visually.

The type of ability measured by this test is useful in occupations where inspection is one of the job elements. It has been found to be important in many assembly-line jobs. It also has been found to play a part in some complex engineering activities where inspection of detail is an important element.

In the TALENT Object Inspection Test, each problem consists of pictures of five small objects, four of which are supposed to be identical. The remaining one is slightly different. The task is to pick out the picture that is different.

A sample item follows:

Item 117.

A   B   C   D   E

(The answer is D.)

THE PREFERENCES TEST

One purpose of this test — frankly an experimental one — is to measure the speed with which a person can reach a decision.

The test is based on a Social Judgments Test developed by the Educational Testing Service.

Each test item consists of a pair of adjectives describing a person. The student is required to select the adjective from each pair that he would prefer to have applicable to his friends. The two characteristics are intended to be about equal in social acceptability.

In considering the results derived from this test, bear in mind that the test is still in the experimental stage of development. We must remember, too, that only one limited kind of decision-making is being tested. This trait may, or may not, be important. We plan to investigate the hypothesis that under some circumstances, the test locates the individual on a continuum that has "snap judgments" at one end and "indecision" at the other.

THEMES

The two five-minute themes were included in the battery for three reasons:

1. They will provide some insight into the student's values, attitudes, personality, motivations, and plans.

2. They will provide a sample of the ability of the student to write coherent and correct English — free of mechanical errors (spelling, punctuation, grammar, etc.), well expressed, and logically organized. It is fully recognized, however, that themes as brief as these, for which only five minutes were allowed, provide an inadequate basis for evaluating the student's ability to produce a well organized composition.

3. They will provide samples of the student's handwriting.

7 The Inventories: Exploring Personality Through Student Activities

In this chapter we trace the beginnings of an instrument designed to measure personality. We become acquainted with Binet and his two daughters; with Rorschach and his inkblots; Woodworth and his Personal Data Sheet. We survey the contributions of Thurstone, Bernreuter, Flanagan, and others to the art of measuring personality. We examine some of the personality tests used most widely today — the Minnesota Multiphasic Personality Inventory, for example — and look at their major strengths and weaknesses.

We end this chapter with a description of the personality test developed for Project TALENT.

About an hour and a half after they had begun, students who took the Project TALENT tests came to a section entitled "Student Activities Inventory."

This section of the tests contained 150 statements, such as "I work fast," "People consider me bold," "I am happy," "I am sensitive," "Most of the time I am considerate." The task before the student was to indicate on the answer sheet whether each statement described him and his usual way of doing things:

> A. extremely well
> B. quite well
> C. fairly well
> D. slightly
> E. not very well.

No doubt the students wondered what such statements had to do with their talents. It is a well known fact, however, that people of equal ability are not always equally successful in life. Why not? Personality differences, we often say. To probe these differences, Project TALENT devised a personality questionnaire to be included along with the aptitude and ability tests.

But what is personality? Before building an assessment device, the TALENT staff had to agree on a definition for personality. This proved to be surprisingly difficult, as the term has many meanings in different situations. For example, one psychologist offered 50 definitions, one of which traced the word back to Roman times and to the Latin word *persona,* meaning "mask." (Masks were used by Roman actors on the stage in connection with the characters they assumed in a play.) For purposes of the Project, personality was finally defined as "the sum of a person's personal characteristics, as indicated by the things he does and his usual way of doing them." Hence the title "Student Activities Inventory" was chosen for the Project TALENT personality questions.

What can we expect to learn from such an inventory? One reason for including a personality inventory in the TALENT battery was based on the hope that it would eventually add to our knowledge of how personality differences help to account for the differences in accomplishments of equally talented normal people. Note that the Project did not attempt to measure abnormalities or psychiatric problems. On the contrary, the inventory was intended for normal individuals, in a search for new information about the way people use their talents and abilities. For example, do people with different kinds of personality patterns plan different kinds of careers? Do they have different educational plans? Do they look for different things in life?

These are only a few examples of the kind of personality information sought by Project TALENT.

Can a personality inventory provide this information? Only
cautious answers are possible. The study of personality has had
limited success. Some researchers, notably G. F. Kuder, of Duke
University, have found that in some cases people in different
jobs are characterized by different patterns of personality traits.
Other studies have shown that personality scores have a low, but
significant, value in predicting success in certain occupations,
such as salesman. These successes, plus evidence gained from
wide use of personality measures in clinical studies, suggest that
personality scores may be related to occupational choices and
successes, but often in less obvious ways than we suppose. Perhaps the results from Project TALENT can tell us how.

Personality inventories are helpful in providing a self-descrip-
tion of a person. True, the student provides the information,
but the test summarizes and categorizes it for him and helps him
to see his own characteristics in a new perspective. Self-descrip-
tion is of limited usefulness if it is available for only one individual, but when the self-descriptions of all of the people in a
group are studied, usable dimensions are brought out for assessing the individual.

2

Before beginning work on the Student Activities Inventory,
the staff reviewed the history of personality measurement — the
problems, mistakes, methods, and successes of others — so that
the TALENT test would be the best product possible.

Personality assessment probably dates back to the earliest history of man, when one cave man estimated that he could bully
another out of the last piece of mammoth meat. From that time
to this, men have been trying to describe and predict the behavior
of other men, for one purpose or another. It was not until the
1880's, however, that Sir Francis Galton, the eminent English
scientist and statistician, developed what might be called the
first personality questionnaire. At the time, however, Galton was
not so much interested in studying personality directly as he
was in studying mental imagery. That is, he was trying to find

out what kinds of mental pictures people get in response to certain kinds of stimuli.

One of the earliest attempts to measure personality specifically was made by the famous French psychologist, Alfred Binet, best known for his Binet Intelligence tests. Binet was born in Nice, France, in 1857. He was educated as a lawyer and physician, but early turned to natural sciences and psychology. He received the degree of Doctor of Science from the Sorbonne in Paris in 1894, and then took over as Director of the Laboratory of Physiological Psychology of the Sorbonne.

One of Binet's most interesting experiments grew out of the study of his two daughters, Marguerite and Armande. From the time they began to walk Binet studied them constantly, observing and taking notes. After they had learned to write, he attempted to categorize their personalities. He began by asking the girls to list words and then to explain their meanings and the images or mental pictures that occurred to them in connection with each word. Marguerite was classified by Binet as an "observer" type since she continually seemed to draw ideas for new words to write by looking at things around her. Marguerite named many things which belonged to her, while Armande listed none. Binet felt that Marguerite was much more concerned with and attached to her possessions than Armande.

In the case of abstractions, the two girls differed considerably. Binet asked each girl to list the articles contained in a house. He noted: "Marguerite visits a *particular* house mentally and names the objects by memory; Armande, on the contrary, thinks of *any* house and names the things that she knows exist in any house." In addition, Armande often made responses which Binet classified as imaginative, while Marguerite's were usually commonplace.

When Binet analyzed the responses of his daughters he found Armande to be introverted and detached from reality; her images were vague and less precise than those of Marguerite. Marguerite's images were concise and vivid and Binet felt that she was extroverted and practical.

Binet also sought — but failed to find — a "ruling factor" or one-word description which would cover the total personality picture of each girl, as revealed by analysis of her responses. In spite of his best efforts, Binet was not able to sum up the total personality picture in terms of one dominant aspect. Thus, the first attempts to assess and define personality by scientific study only succeeded in emphasizing its diversity.

Following Binet, psychologists and educators tried many approaches to the measurement of personality. One which has survived until today is the word association technique of Carl Jung, a Swiss psychologist and psychiatrist. Jung was born in 1875 and lived in Zurich until his death in 1961. Although he eventually broke away to establish his own school of psychological thought, from 1907 to 1912 he was one of the leading disciples of Sigmund Freud. It was Jung's idea that if you asked a person to say the first thing that came into his mind, his response would reveal something about his personality. Since this method was somewhat awkward, and many of the responses were difficult to interpret, Jung decided that he would make up a list of carefully selected words and ask people to say the first thing they thought of as he presented each word. People's varied responses to the same list of words, Jung reasoned, should provide an index to differences in personality. In the standard series of 100 words, a number of potentially emotional words, such as "love," are mixed in with neutral words such as "house" and "box." The interpretation of the responses to such word lists is complex, however, and this technique of personality measurement has found favor primarily in the clinical treatment of individual patients.

Another early form of personality measurement which has persisted to the present time is the Inkblot Technique of Hermann Rorschach, another Swiss physician and psychiatrist. Born in Zurich in 1884, Rorschach became interested in inkblots shortly after receiving his medical degree in 1910. He felt that abnormal people had characteristic ways of seeing things, depending on the nature of their problems, and he felt that there was need for a way to measure these characteristics. He used inkblots because they contained no particular designs, and this allowed his patients the maximum opportunity to display their own personalities in their responses. In presenting the inkblots to his subjects, Rorschach simply said something like: "People see all sorts of things in these inkblot pictures; now tell me what *you* see. What does each inkblot make you think of?" After ten years of experimentation, Rorschach published his findings, including the set of inkblots now called the Rorschach Test, in a monograph called

Psychodiagnostik. Only a few months later he died at the age of 37.

The idea of using ambiguous words or pictures or inkblots so that the person responding would have the maximum chance to give responses characteristic of himself came to be quite popular. Today, in addition to the Rorschach method, we have many others based upon similar ideas. These are often grouped under the name of "projective" techniques because they give the patient a chance to "project" or display his own personality when he tells what the stimulus makes him think of or what he sees.

The methods of Binet, which might be called "case studies," and the projective methods of Jung and Rorschach are still popular. However they are designed primarily for the clinical study of the individual. Project TALENT required a method which would be adaptable to the study of the personality of large numbers of students in a short time. For this reason, among others, Project TALENT chose to use the questionnaire or inventory technique. In this technique the student marks his choice of several ways in which each of a list of statements might describe him. This type of personality inventory is often called a "self-report" inventory, since the student reports his own answers to questions about himself.

Although Sir Francis Galton had pioneered in the use of the inventory in his studies of mental images back in the 1880's, the use of the self-report or personality inventory on a large scale did not begin to come into its own until World War I. At that time, the armed services were inducting men in wholesale numbers. A strong need arose for diagnosing the ability of recruits to adjust themselves satisfactorily to the rigors and strains of military life. Obviously, it was not possible for military psychologists to interview every man drafted. The need was for a quick, paper-and-pencil type of screening device which could be given to large groups of draftees by relatively untrained people. To fill this need, Robert S. Woodworth developed the first of the large-scale, group personality tests, his famous Personal Data Sheet.

Woodworth was born in 1869, in Belchertown, Massachusetts. His childhood ambitions ran the gamut from astronomer through farmer, musician, and philosopher. After graduating from college, he taught mathematics and science. Fully 12 years after graduation he settled on psychology as his chosen field.

In 1917, Woodworth was asked by the American Psychological Association to develop the Personal Data Sheet for the Army. He studied the symptoms of war neuroses, then called "shell shock," and examined case histories of neurosis from the files of neurologists and psychiatrists. He conferred with prominent psychiatrists. Following these investigations he constructed a series of questions concerning symptoms which were characteristic of, or might lead to, war neuroses. The questions, which could be answered by "Yes" or "No," were generally of two types: those referring to the past history of the subject and those referring to his present behavior. If a person's score was poor compared to the normal group, neurotic symptoms were assumed to be indicated. A psychiatric interview was then arranged for the person. Woodworth intended the Personal Data Sheet only as a device to screen out the "worst bets" for military service. It was quite successful for its purpose. This inventory was the first widely used example of the questionnaire-inventory approach to personality assessment, and it set the pattern for many similar questionnaires following the war.

The impetus which the war gave to psychological measures in general, along with the success of Woodworth's Personal Data Sheet, resulted in a flurry of new inventories for personality assessment. Many of these were direct outgrowths of the Personal Data Sheet, both in form and content. Some of them introduced one or more minor changes in Woodworth's procedures. Most confined themselves to the measurement of single traits such as "neuroticism," "emotional stability," or "introversion-extroversion." Many variations of the "Yes-No" type of answer were tried with little significant improvement. Efforts to improve personality inventories continued, however, and the use of methods for relating items both to total score on the inventory and to measures outside of the test itself were important technical improvements.

The rapid growth of personality studies soon led to efforts to combine measures of several different traits or dimensions into one "multi-dimensional" inventory. Some multi-dimensional inventories were no more than several of the old one-trait inventories bound in one booklet. Each trait being measured had its own separate set of questions or items in the booklet. However, a young Stanford University graduate student working on his doctor's degree wondered if it might not be possible to find a set of questions which could be scored in several different ways so that several traits would be measured with the same items. In exploring this idea, Robert G. Bernreuter developed the test that bears his name and which is still one of the most widely used personality inventories.

Bernreuter's Personality Inventory was first published in 1931. It consisted of only 125 "Yes" and "No" questions drawn from a much larger pool of items in four earlier one-trait tests. The inventory was intended to measure simultaneously the four traits measured by these tests — "neurotic tendency," "self-sufficiency," "introversion-extroversion," and "dominance-submission." Each of the 125 items was scored as part of each of the four scales. About 400 university students were given the four original sets of questions and Bernreuter's new inventory. Bernreuter demonstrated that the four scores derived from the items in his inventory provided very adequate substitutes for the four scores from the separate inventories. This supported his idea that one set of items can serve several purposes at one time.

Bernreuter's Inventory had only been out about three years when, as a graduate student at Harvard University, John C. Flanagan began to cast about for a topic for his doctoral dissertation. At this time there was great pressure from many sides to make psychology a more quantitative science. Statisticians such as Godfrey Thomson and Charles Spearman, in England, and Truman Kelley, Karl Holzinger, Harold Hotelling, and L. L. Thurstone, in America, were working with a new statistical technique called "factor analysis."[1] Flanagan, who was studying with Truman Kelley, hit upon the idea of applying factor analysis to Bernreuter's Inventory. Bernreuter had selected four personality traits and had provided scores on each. Flanagan gave the test again and applied factor analysis. The results showed that only two scales, one which he called Self-Confidence and one

[1] Factor analysis is a statistical technique for mathematically identifying important dimensions or traits. If a number of tests or measures are related to each other, this inter-relationship means that each measure has something in common with the others. This common element is called a "factor." Factor analysis seeks to sort out and measure the common elements which underlie related measures. Many times such factors are more basic and important than the measures themselves. Many times measuring only a few factors yields as much information as giving a large number of somewhat related tests. (See, for example: Holzinger, K. J. and Harmon, H. H., *Factor Analysis*. Chicago: U. of Chicago Press, 1941).

which he called Sociability, included nearly all the information in Bernreuter's four test scores.

Flanagan's work started a new line of development in personality assessment. (It also earned him his doctor's degree from Harvard University in 1934.) Following Flanagan's success in applying factor analysis to personality measurements, a number of instruments were developed using the factor-analytic approach. Those in favor of this approach have argued that factor analysis permits the description of human behavior in terms of a relatively few independent, basic dimensions. Those favoring other approaches often feel that factor analysis is too mathematical, leaving the "person" out of "personality." Nevertheless, factor-based inventories continue to appear.

A good example of these are the three inventories developed by J. P. Guilford, between 1936 and 1939. Whereas Flanagan's application of factor analysis to the Bernreuter Inventory was based on the relationships (intercorrelations) among the four scores on the inventory, Guilford analyzed the relationships among *items*. This process enabled him to use factor analysis in grouping items to form his scales initially, rather than revising or rearranging scales previously developed.

Some of the most extensive research to date using factor analysis in personality evaluation has been carried out at the University of Illinois by English-born R. B. Cattell, who received his doctorate from the University of London in 1929. A number of important points about Cattell's work should be mentioned. First, he has set up a systematic plan for investigating the area of personality assessment. Second, he has rejected the idea of traits alone, insisting that they must always be considered in terms of the conditions or situation immediately present. Finally, he has distinguished between "surface" traits and "source" traits — source traits corresponding to forces deep within the personality. According to Cattell, what we observe as the personality of an individual are his "surface" traits which spring from the underlying source traits. Source traits can only be discovered by mathematical analysis and psychological insight, since they cannot be observed directly as can the surface traits.

Cattell has devised a number of tests to measure the factors that he has identified in his studies. Two examples are the Sixteen Personality Factor Questionnaire and the Objective-Analytic

Personality Test Batteries. While these tests seem promising in many respects, they require that the user be thoroughly grounded in Cattell's complex system of concepts, terms, and theories.

Factor analysis has provided one avenue of development in personality questionnaires, but progress has also been made in the development and improvement of non-factor inventories. One non-factor method for developing new inventories, called "empirical keying," was introduced about 1940. This method consists of giving a large number of questions to groups of people of each kind that you hope to be able to identify through the inventory (for instance certain neurotics and schizophrenics.) All the questions are given to each group and also to a large number of people representing the general population. The results are studied, and only those questions that distinguish each group from all other groups and from people in general are kept in the test. Sets of questions have thus been selected which can sort out people of various kinds who differ from people in general.

One of the most widely used personality inventories, the Minnesota Multiphasic Personality Inventory, was constructed in 1940 by means of "empirical keying." This test was designed by Starke R. Hathaway and J. C. McKinley of the University of Minnesota to identify people with various kinds of mental illness. Hathaway and McKinley tried out over 1000 questions in order to find about half that number which would satisfactorily sort out people with different types of mental illness.

While the post-World War I boom in personality inventories has slowed down somewhat, a great deal of work still goes on in the field. There is active interest in the area on the part of educators, psychologists, and the general public. Nevertheless, almost from the beginning, paper-and-pencil personality inventories have been under criticism for one reason or another. The main criticisms of the self-report type of personality inventory center around four areas:

The first of these is *frankness*. Critics charge that people do not always provide an open and honest picture of themselves. They say most people are able to fake their responses in some particular way if it seems advantageous to do so; and even those who don't fake them willingly may unwittingly present a distorted picture of themselves.

The second might be called *self-insight*. In order to be able to respond with true information about himself, a person must first be aware of his true nature. Studies have repeatedly shown — and personal experiences bear this out — that people often aren't aware of their personal quirks and defects, and thus can hardly be expected to report them in response to a question.

The next involves *reading load*. Inventories often run to several hundred questions. A poor reader, after struggling with this load for a while, may give up in his attempt to understand each question and answer an unpredictable number of them superficially, or even at random.

Lastly, criticism has to do with *focus*. Many inventories are focused on abnormality. Relatively few inventories have been produced for the purpose of describing the personalities of normal, everyday people.

On the positive side of the ledger, the personality inventory has the great practical value of serving as a formalized interview. It is objective and standardized; it is relatively inexpensive; it makes relatively low demands on the time of those who take and those who give the inventory; and it is easy to score. Furthermore, many studies show that inventories are moderately effective in differentiating between various groups. Finally, improvements are being made in many directions that appear to hold promise of additional progress in the future.

In closing our review of the "state of the art" in personality assessment, it is perhaps well to mention two of a number of recent improvements which appear promising. One, aimed at the problem of "frankness," is called the "forced choice" technique.

Many studies have demonstrated that people could present an unreal view of themselves when this seemed desirable to them. This situation is particularly bad when a person may have something to gain by presenting a false picture of himself, as in the case of someone applying for a job in industry or seeking promotion in military life. In response to such criticisms, several psychologists in the mid-1940's developed the "forced choice technique." In this technique, the subject is required to choose between two alternative statements or answers which appear equally desirable or acceptable, but which differ with respect to their scoring weights for the trait really being measured. By requiring a relative rather than an absolute judgment, the forced choice item tends to reduce the ambiguity usually associated with terms such as "often," "rarely," and "well." In addition, "fakability" is reduced, although it is not eliminated. Whenever the person who takes the test has a strong reason to present himself in a particular light, he can usually do so to some extent. Where there is little reason to fake, the traditional self-report type of inventory is sometimes preferable by virtue of its simplicity and understandability.

A second type of improvement being made lies in the development of "control" scores for tests to show when the test results are not trustworthy. One of the most important innovations of the Minnesota Multiphasic Personality Inventory was a set of four "control" scales which attempt to show the extent to which the person taking the test tried to give a false impression of himself. While these four control scales have not been completely successful, they have contributed greatly to the success of this inventory.

In summary, personality assessment has shown a steady growth since 1918. Both factor-based and non-factor tests have flourished as a result of increased efficiency, refinement, and new ideas. Many specific devices have been developed to meet the criticisms advanced on the grounds of lack of frankness and insight, heavy reading load, and often inappropriate focus. Devices such as forced choice and control scores have not been uniformly successful, but do hold promise for the improvement of already useful measures.

3

In designing the TALENT personality inventory we drew upon our historical review, tailoring our conclusions to fit the needs of the Project. Thus, the TALENT Student Activities Inventory was essentially self-administering, not very time consuming, and adaptable to machine scoring and computer analysis. In general, the inventory was one which represented the "state of the art" in assessing the personality of normal individuals.

The first point we considered was the type of inventory to be used. A form which would assess many traits at once was needed. But should it be a collection of trait measures where each item is scored for just one trait, or should it be of the Bernreuter type? The latter type is more efficient since several scores may be obtained from the same set of items simply by scoring the items differently for each trait included. This efficiency is somewhat offset, however, by the fact that the scores obtained from such an inventory may appear to show some inter-relationships between two traits simply because the *same items* are scored for the two traits, not necessarily because the inter-relationship actually exists between the traits themselves. Flanagan has shown that such artificial relationships are often of little importance and that statistical corrections can be applied to eliminate them. Nevertheless, they introduce complications, so it was decided that each item should be written and scored for just one trait.

Other refinements such as the use of forced choice and control scales were considered. However, these are most useful where there is reason to believe that people may try to fake their answers. Since the students tested by Project TALENT would have little reason for faking, it was decided to keep the test as simple as possible in the interests of reducing reading load and making it easier to understand.

Another problem was just what to include. The inventory might have been designed to describe traits identified through logical and psychological analysis; or it might have been designed for traits identified through a statistical procedure, such as factor analysis. Both approaches have advantages and limitations, so it was decided to combine some of the features of both. Personality is often revealed by the things people do — *the way they behave*. Since Project TALENT was interested in high school students, high school behaviors defined the contents of the personality scales.

Further, the Project staff decided that it would use behavioral adjectives to represent high school behaviors. That is, adjectives describing the way high school people behave and act would form the basic raw material of the inventory. (A behavioral adjective tells something about a student's *behavior* as opposed to simply describing his appearance — for instance, "friendly," "helpful," "aggressive," rather than "tall," "dark," and "handsome.")

Several sources of behavioral adjectives were examined (one contained almost 18,000 adjectives). It was clear that many of the behaviors described, such as "senile," "hen-pecked," "care-worn," and so on, were not appropriate for high school students. Therefore, the behaviors were selected in accordance with the following four criteria:

1. The behavior occurs in high school and is observable.
2. It can be defined well enough to be identified by a high school student.
3. It is reasonable to expect a high school student to be able to rate himself on this behavior.
4. The behavior can be expected to be importantly related to future behavior.

When a sample of behavioral adjectives had been drawn and sifted according to these criteria, about 2,000 words remained. We analyzed these very carefully, and behaviors which seemed to go together logically and psychologically were grouped together and called a "trait." Since care was used to group only those behaviors which were very close to each other, these traits were later called "narrow traits." In order to define these traits practically, and to assist in writing statements to measure them, each narrow trait was further identified by specifying a few of the original behavioral adjectives which seemed most typical of it. For example, the trait called "impulsiveness" was typified by adjectives such as "impulsive," "hasty," and "impetuous." The trait called "vigor" was typified by adjectives such as "vigorous," "active," and "forceful." While the narrow traits identified through this process did not cover all the kinds of things high school students do, they did sample a wide range of high school behaviors. Further study convinced the staff that sampling of narrow traits, or combinations of such samples, would be related quite highly to the important aspects of personality such as dominance, sociability, self-confidence, etc., often found by using complex statistical methods such as factor analysis. The narrow traits also seemed more appropriate in the Project TALENT

situation than factor-based or other more complicated procedures.

Once the traits were decided upon, items were prepared for
each of the traits. These items were simple statements about the
various high school activities or behaviors which were associated
with the traits. The typical adjectives for the traits were used as
guides in writing the statements. For example, the adjective
"hasty" leads to the statement "I often do things on the spur of
the moment"; "impulsive" leads to "I am an impulsive person";
"tireless" leads to "I can work or play for hours without getting
tired." In the inventory, students were asked to indicate how well
such statements would describe them and their own behavior by
checking: (A) extremely well, (B) quite well, (C) fairly well,
(D) slightly, or (E) not very well. Thus, the sum of their answers to the set of statements associated with a particular trait
gave a descriptive score for that trait.

As was the case with all other measuring instruments of
Project TALENT, we first developed a preliminary form of the
inventory. Statements were written for a preliminary set of 18
traits shown below:

Leadership	Impulsiveness
Vigor	Persistence
Productivity	Calmness
Tidiness	Social Adjustment
Sociability	Theoreticality
Self-Confidence	Responsibility
Cheerfulness	Social Sensitivity
Culture	Group-Centeredness
Talkativeness	Conventionalism

(See Appendix, Section D, for a description and sample statement for each trait.)

A preliminary form of the inventory, based on this first set of
traits, was given to several hundred high school students. The
results were carefully studied and some of the statements and
traits were eliminated. In other cases, traits were combined.
This resulted in the final version of the inventory, which consists
of a total of 150 statements, including the 10 traits shown in
Table 3.

TABLE 3

Traits Measured in Student Activities Inventory

Trait	Number of Statements	Preliminary Traits from which Derived
1. Sociability	12	Sociability and Cheerfulness
2. Social Sensitivity	9	Social Sensitivity
3. Impulsiveness	9	Impulsiveness
4. Vigor	7	Vigor
5. Calmness	9	Calmness
6. Tidiness	11	Tidiness
7. Culture	10	Culture and Manners
8. Leadership	5	Leadership
9. Self-Confidence	12	Self-Confidence
10 Mature Personality	24	Productivity, Persistence, and Responsibility
Unscored Statements	42	All traits
Total	150	

The traits measured in the final form of the inventory do not cover the entire range of high school personality. However, the 150 statements are related to more personality characteristics than the 10 traits scored in the final form of the inventory. Undoubtedly the information accumulated as a result of the TALENT personality inventory will aid substantially in setting up a sound basis for predicting the future behavior and achievements of American high school students.

8   The Inventories:
Probing the Student's
Vocational Interests

This chapter deals with the second of the inventories developed for Project TALENT, namely, the vocational interest inventory. As in the previous chapter, we first trace the beginnings of interest measurement, and then describe the most widely used instruments today — those of Strong and Kuder.

Because the measurement of vocational interests is still a new (and sometimes misunderstood) practice, we point out the uses and possible abuses of interest inventories. We conclude the chapter by describing how we went about devising, testing, and perfecting the vocational interest inventory for Project TALENT.

As the second half-day of the testing began, students focused their attention on a set of questions designed to measure their relative interest in occupations which ranged from bookkeeper and bankteller to U.S. Senator and President of the United States. The student's task was to indicate the degree of interest he or she had in each of 122 occupations. The directions told the student that for each type of work listed he was to mark one of the following choices:

> "A. I would *like* this *very much*
> B. I would *like* this *fairly well*
> C. *Indifferent* or *don't know much about it*
> D. I would *dislike* this a *little*
> E. I would *dislike* this *very much*"

After working through the list of occupations, students were asked to indicate similar degrees of interest in 82 activities — from fishing, operating a power engine, buying stock, or hiring and firing people, to campaigning for office.

This stock-taking of interests required no more than 20 minutes. Yet behind this 20-minute inventory lay a long history of scientific effort.

2

Scientists began the measurement of interests early in the century when a number of psychologists became aware of the significance of interests as an important aspect of human behavior. To a group of men at the Carnegie Institute of Technology in Pittsburgh the time appeared ripe for new applications of psychology to the educational and vocational problems of individuals. The groundwork for measuring human behavior had been laid in previous decades. Alfred Binet and Charles Spearman had studied the measurement of intelligence and had constructed a number of instruments for that purpose. Many other psychologists were contributing tests and ideas. But perhaps the strongest impetus to the measurement movement came from the group testing of intelligence with the Army Alpha and Beta Tests during World War I. These tests demonstrated that scientifically devised instruments could be applied successfully to large numbers of people. Following the 1918 armistice, many psychologists returned to their universities and research posts eager to discover new ways of applying psychological measurements in education, industry, and commerce.

It was the group gathered together by Walter V. Bingham at the Carnegie Institute of Technology that contributed most to our understanding of interests. These scientists approached the measurement of interests as their colleagues had approached the measurement of intelligence and personality — with objectivity, logic, and above all with respect for facts. Here a number of important ideas were germinated and some of the early interest inventories came into being. Credit goes to Edward K. Strong, Jr., for a sustained study program which was largely responsible for developing interest measurement to its present state. He developed a self-rating inventory of interests in occupations, school subjects, amusements, activities and people. Strong later directed the work of Karl M. Cowdery, a graduate student at Stanford University, on problems in interest measurement.

Strong's device was his Vocational Interest Blank — used effectively in industry for 30 years to select qualified personnel from among a large number of applicants. A notable example of its early use was by the Life Insurance Agency Management Association. This organization was concerned with the rapid turnover of life insurance salesmen — newly hired salesmen seemed to quit almost as rapidly as they were hired. Research workers reasoned that if it were possible to screen out applicants who had little chance to succeed as salesmen, training costs as well as turnover would be reduced. Among a number of instruments tested for screening applicants was Strong's Vocational Interest Blank. For a time, each new applicant was asked to fill out the blank; and, for purposes of evaluating the instrument, none was rejected on the basis of his answers. The scores were filed until a number of the men had had an opportunity to accumulate sales experience. Then the results of the interest blank were brought out and compared to effectiveness in terms of sales. The research workers found that men who, as applicants, had scored high on Strong's Life Insurance Salesmen scale were usually the same men who sold the greatest amount of life insurance. With this justification, Strong's instrument was adopted to screen future sales applicants.

To improve our understanding of the role of interests, Strong began a long-range study of the effects of human interests and their relation to educational and vocational pursuits. He asked whether interests are, in fact, a lasting and stable quality of the individual, or whether they are reflections of passing moods and inclinations. If interests are highly changeable over the years, he reasoned, then the utility of interest measurement for vocational and educational guidance would be limited. In 1943, Dr. Strong published *Vocational Interests of Men and Women,* and in 1955, *Vocational Interests Eighteen Years After College.* These two books and many articles published in professional journals established the lasting and stable quality of the interests measured by his inventory.

Another interest blank, familiar to parents and teachers of high school children, was developed by Frederic Kuder while at the Ohio State University. One of the major differences between Strong's Interest Blank and Kuder's Preference Record is in the type of scores offered. Strong's Interest Blank provides scores for comparing the individual's interests with those of successful men and women in specific occupations — artist, psychologist, lawyer, professional athlete, etc. Kuder's Preference Record provides interest scores in broader families of occupations, such as science, mechanics, clerical work, or the arts.

Guidance experts recommend the use of interest tests of these types but suggest that the scores be interpreted with caution until more data accumulate regarding the development and functioning of interest patterns.

3

There are a number of points to note about interest inventories, now that we have seen something of their development.

1. Different inventories provide different results. It is not unusual for counselors to ask students to complete two inventories, since the information gained from one will not necessarily cover the same areas as the information gained from another. As we have seen, Strong's Vocational Interest Blank will indicate interest in various specific occupations; Kuder's Preference Record, on the other hand, provides scores in broader areas, such as scientific, literary, or musical fields.

2. The interests of young people may be expected to change, particularly when they are in the ninth and tenth grades. At this age, boys and girls are maturing. One week Johnny wants to become an engineer and the next week a lawyer. Quite often Johnny needs to become more familiar with different occupa-

tions before his interests become stable. When children are at this age, the results of interest inventories should not be interpreted as suggesting a final occupational choice.

For college students and mature high school students in the 11th and 12th grades, the results of interest inventories are likely to be more trustworthy indications of long-term interests.

3. Interests are not the same as aptitudes or abilities. A high score on scientific interests does not necessarily mean that the lad who obtained it could be a scientist. He may not have the ability to do well in science or mathematics courses. However, if Johnny scores high on scientific and mechanical interests, but is only an average student in school, he might choose to become a technician or machinist. Both of these occupations are associated with interest in science and mechanics. Interests are sometimes thought of as providing *direction,* and ability as setting the *level of accomplishment* likely to be reached.

4. Interest inventories are used primarily for educational and vocational purposes. Rarely do they become involved with broad personal values and attitudes. An interest inventory tells us little about an adolescent's attitudes toward government or religion.

5. Only a qualified guidance counselor or psychologist should be consulted for a detailed interpretation of the scores from an interest inventory. He will be familiar with many different inventories (we have discussed only two out of more than thirty such inventories now available) and will be able to point out to the student the implications of the scores. He will also take into account the child's school performance, aptitude and ability test scores, and personality.

4

Interest inventories have definitely shown promise, and in spite of uncertainties regarding the interpretation of such types of scores, our advisory panels recommended an interest inventory as one of the instruments for inclusion in Project TALENT. Interests, as mainsprings for individual action and success, represent an important national resource. And, since Project TALENT was to be a census of the talents of our youth, we felt that the inclusion of an interest survey was essential to provide information useful for national planning. Information on interests on a national scale would give us clues as to how many boys would like to become scientists, lawyers, mechanics, or enter politics. We would learn how many girls would like to become nurses, dietitians, or teachers. And, we would learn even more by finding out how many of our youth interested in each occupation also appeared to have the requisite abilities to succeed in it.

In short, Project TALENT was here taking advantage of an opportunity to look at expressed interests in conjunction with abilities, personal background, and activities; and to discover the importance of adolescents' interests in relation to later success.

When we began the task of constructing the TALENT Interest Inventory, we first examined and evaluated the published inventories, including the Strong and Kuder instruments. We decided to devise a new inventory, designed to fit the special needs of our study.

The first question confronting us was whether to devise a measure using a rating scale or a ranking method. On a rating scale, the student expresses his liking, disliking, or indifference to each occupation or activity presented, as in the following example:

> For each occupation listed below, you are to consider whether or not you would like that kind of work. . . . Mark your answers as follows:
>
> A. I would like this very much.
> B. I would like this fairly well.
> C. Indifferent or don't know much about it.
> D. I would dislike this a little.
> E. I would dislike this very much.
>
> 1. Surgeon
> 2. Chemist
> 3. Civil engineer
> 4. Writer
> 5. Social worker

A ranking procedure presents several occupations or activities together and asks the student to choose the one that he likes the most and the one that he likes the least, as in the following example:

For each group of occupations listed below, indicate the one you would like most and the one you would like least:

A. Mathematician
B. Machinist
C. Dietitian

We preferred the rating procedure because it would enable us to report how many students in the country would like to become surgeons, auto mechanics, teachers, and so on. A ranking procedure, we felt, would confuse the issue because the student would be forced to choose among alternatives. Moreover, it would not yield information on how many young people might like to become surgeons, for example, but only on how many would prefer being a surgeon to being a lawyer.

Several experimental forms, using the agreed-upon rating procedure, were written by the staff and reviewed by our advisory panels. One was selected and tried out with more than 600 students in two high schools and one university freshman class. From this try-out, we found that we could reduce the number of questions from 300 to 205 without limiting the scope of the inventory. We found, too, that our inventory was easily understood and readily accepted by the students.

We developed the TALENT Interest Inventory solely for research purposes. Results were not returned to the participating schools, since the Inventory was not as yet tested for practical use.

In later research studies, we will investigate the role that interests play in the achievement of educational goals. We will explore interests for what they tell us about the student's prospects for college. For example, does interest in academic work necessarily predict success in college? What effect do interests have on a student's grades, on his choice of an occupation, and on his subsequent success in his chosen career? Does the person who has a clear concept of his interests make a more intelligent occupational choice than the person who lacks such a concept? Research on these and many other questions involving interests is sparse and contradictory. But as a result of Project TALENT we now have a large reservoir of information which should shed new light on this important area of human behavior.

9   The Inventories:
Stocktaking of Experiences
and Influences

The third inventory developed for Project TALENT was designed to search for the background and contemporary forces affecting youth's plans, drives, and aspirations. We called it the Student Information Blank. Few instruments of similar scope and probing-depth had ever been developed before. We list the type of facts this blank sought from the students and provide a few examples of the questions to which students were asked to respond.

This chapter concludes the description of the three inventories.

Every minute of test time is a precious resource in an undertaking involving nearly half a million individuals. Yet, we decided to allot 80 minutes to a task which did not measure the student's fund of subject matter, but rather sought information about his personal experiences, his home and family, his hopes and aspirations. Why? Our purpose was to explore the impact of these factors on school achievement, educational goals, occupational choices and success. The importance of personal background is recognized — witness such quotations from literature as "What is past is prologue," "Just as the twig is bent, the tree's inclined," "The child is father of the man." All attest to the molding force of past experience.

The instrument we used to gather data about students' past experience was the Student Information Blank, designed specifically for Project TALENT. The directions read, in part: "This is not a test, and there are no right or wrong answers. . . ." The Student Information Blank was neither a test nor an inventory from which summary scores were to be obtained. It was a quest for a body of background information that is destined to play an important role in future research.

2

In the long run, Project TALENT is not only interested in the abilities and current level of achievement of the youth of our country, but also in whether our young people put their talents to good use for themselves and society. Certainly, many factors enter into a student's educational and occupational plans, and whether he carries them to fruition. Sometimes these have little to do with his talent or ability, but instead are related to his personal background — for instance, the economic status of his family, the cultural climate of his home, the neighborhood in which he lives, or the hobbies that are available to him.

As the focal point, we decided to seek information on those matters of background which have been shown to have a relationship to three pivotal occurrences in a young person's life — whether he drops out of high school or stays until graduation; whether he enters college and succeeds or fails; and why he makes a choice of one occupation rather than another.

One great waste of talent in our nation is the large number of boys and girls who do not complete high school. Most states have a compulsory attendance law, requiring attendance until children reach 16 years of age. But at 16, many boys and girls drop out of school, even though it is increasingly important for them to have a high school education in order to earn an adequate income and to contribute as responsible citizens. One research study found that youths who dropped out of high school usually had failed subjects in elementary school; were frequently absent from class; had low scholastic aptitudes; were often discipline problems; ordinarily did not participate in school activities; and lacked a feeling of identification with the school. Other studies have shown that school drop-outs are often older than their classmates and come from lower socio-economic backgrounds.

Despite the high rate of high school drop-outs, an increasing proportion of our youth go on to college. Our next question, then, is: What characteristics distinguish youths who enter college from those who do not? Previous studies suggest that college-bound students have above-average ability and scholastic achievement, and that their families are less often in the lowest economic bracket. The father's occupation, the parents' views on the importance of a college education, the parents' willingness and ability to provide financial support — all these play a part in determining whether a youth will enroll and stay in college or turn to other pursuits after high school. Other significant factors are the student's own values (does he see college as a step toward his goals?); his social contacts (are his friends going to college?); his proximity to a college (is there one within commuting distance?).

What backgrounds and experiences lead to the decision to enter and the motivation to succeed in various occupations? The Bureau of the Census gives us information that shows the relationship of various jobs and incomes (one measure of success) to age, sex, and education. Studies aimed at selection of promising employees often give us a picture of background elements that appear to be related to success in particular occupations. But many questions are still unanswered. For example, what relationship exists between the father's occupation and the occupation chosen by a son or daughter? Do American parents stress bettering one's position so that the child's occupational aspirations are higher than his father's? What role does occupational guidance in high school and college play? How do the age at which a person marries and the number of children he has affect both his choice of occupation and his success in it?

From the point of view of education and guidance, the problem is to reduce the number of poor choices that are made so that students do not waste time on inappropriate training or in trying to succeed in an occupation ill-suited to their capabilities. One of the purposes of the Student Information Blank was to collect information that would help identify the forces that cause young people to enter one occupation rather than another. To what extent are these forces storm winds, prevailing winds, whimsical breezes, or merely doldrums?

3

We developed the TALENT Student Information Blank by accumulating a list of questions about students' personal experiences, family and home backgrounds, and plans for the future that appeared to be relevant to the research purposes of the study. Each question was screened for clarity and questions were written and rewritten until pilot interviews with students showed them to be clear. In selecting the final set of questions, the advisory panels and the staff were influenced by the extent to which previous research had established the question as an important one. The final questionnaire asked 394 questions.

The questions were largely objective, asking about verifiable facts or events rather than for subjective reports of personal feelings. Students were not required to write their answers, but to select one of several responses and to indicate their selection on the answer sheet. The responses were written to offer two to 36 choices, depending on the question. We found that answers to most questions could be adequately covered by allowing only five or six response categories.

Examples of the final forms of the questions are shown in three specific questions which sought evidence of leadership experience, work experience, and social experience:

How many times have you been president of a class, a club, or other organization in the last three years?

    A. None
    B. Once
    C. Twice
    D. Three times
    E. Four times
    F. Five or more times

During the school year, about how many hours a week do you work for pay?

A. None
B. About 1–5 hours
C. About 6–10 hours
D. About 11–15 hours
E. About 16–20 hours
F. About 21 hours or more

On the average, how many evenings a week during the school year do you usually go out for fun and recreation?

A. Less than one
B. One
C. Two
D. Three
E. Four or five
F. Six or seven

Below is a description of the questions that were included in the Student Information Blank, and some of the reasons for asking them. Because the questions are of a personal nature, every step has been taken to assure complete anonymity — under no circumstances will the name of any student be disclosed. The sole purpose in asking these questions is to study the patterns of experience and background that contribute to avocational and vocational growth. The questions are grouped under Personal Experiences, Family and Home, and Plans for the Future. The first group of questions, dealing with personal experiences, covered the following topics:

1. Organizations — number and kind of clubs joined; offices held. Membership in school clubs is one indication that a student is not likely to drop out of school.

2. Hobbies and recreational activities. Voluntary activities not only indicate an individual's interests, but they sometimes lead to a choice of an occupation.

3. Work experiences — amount of time worked during the school year and summer; types of jobs held. These questions were designed to enable us to study the effect of work experience during high school years on adjustment to later employment.

4. Sources of personal income — per cent of spending money

coming from allowances from home and from jobs. Source of spending money may reflect initiative and independence.

5. Dating and social activities. Answers may give some indication of a youngster's social development.

6. Reading — number of books read; types of reading (adventure, science fiction, biography). Reading is sometimes indicative of interests that relate to educational and vocational choices.

7. Studying — number of hours per week spent studying; study habits. Research has shown that study habits are related to scholastic achievement. Here are a few of the questions we asked:

"For the following statements indicate how often each one applies to you. . . . Mark one of the following choices for each statement:

    A. Almost always
    B. Most of the time
    C. About half the time
    D. Not very often
    E. Almost never

• I make sure that I understand what I am to do before I start an assignment.

• My teachers have criticized me for turning in a sloppy assignment.

• I pronounce the words to myself as I am reading.

• When studying for a test, I am able to pick out important points to learn.

• I don't seem to be able to concentrate on what I read. My mind wanders and many things distract me."

8. Schooling — courses taken, grades earned, transfers from school to school, amount of time missed from school. Such matters should relate to entry into college and achievement in college.

9. Guidance and counseling experiences — how often students seek vocational and educational help and from whom. Such questions should reveal what persons are influential in helping

a youngster make educational and occupational plans, and whether school guidance facilities are being used.

10. Awards — academic, artistic, athletic, or organizational honors. These may be a factor in a student's educational and vocational development.

11. Driving — whether instructed at school; when; how often a car is available. The last fact may be particularly significant in studying the student's use of time.

12. Health. The purpose of questions about health was to identify students whose health might limit their educational and vocational opportunities.

Next, the Information Blank sought facts about the family and home — data needed if we were to assess the influence of home environment on educational and occupational development. The areas covered were as follows:

1. Family composition — who made up the student's family, including father, mother, brothers and sisters, grandparents, other relatives; whether the student was a twin or triplet.

2. Parent's occupation. These questions were crucial ones, since there is evidence of a strong relationship between the father's job and a child's performance in school, whether the student goes to college, and his choice of career.

3. Education of family members — including schooling of parents, brothers and sisters.

4. Economic status — estimate of total family income; major source of income. With this information we can roughly establish the ability of the family to support the student while in college and perhaps make a study of the need for scholarships. This will also provide facts that will enable us to relate economic situation to school achievement, and to educational and career choices.

5. Description of home — type (house or apartment); amount of rent paid or value of building; number and type of appliances and furnishings. Results here will provide supplementary data on economic situation.

6. Family mobility — number and frequency of house to house or region to region moves. Questions about mobility, as well as other questions about the home (above), will help us measure the influence of home conditions on the student.

7. Foreign languages spoken by parents. Here we wanted to

find out if a student whose parents speak a foreign language has a better chance than others to excel in foreign languages.

8. Books and magazines in the home. As one indication of the cultural level of the home we asked:

How many books are in your home?

A. None, or very few (0–10)
B. A few books (11–25)
C. One bookcase full (26–100)
D. Two bookcases full (101–250)
E. Three or four bookcases full (251–500)
F. A room full — a library (501 or more)

Past research has shown that children from homes with many books attend college in greater proportion than do children from homes with few books.

9. Automobiles owned. The number of automobiles owned by anyone in the home provides an indication of the opportunity for a student to learn to drive or to repair a car. It also gives an indication of economic status.

Finally, the Information Blank asked questions about the students' plans and aspirations for the future.

1. Educational plans. Was the student planning to quit high school? Did he plan to attend college — full time or part time? Would he attend a trade, vocational, or business school? Students also were asked to express their reasons for or against going to college.

2. Specific college plans. These questions, asked only of 11th and 12th grade students, dealt with choice of college course, type of college they expected to attend, the number of colleges to which they had applied, and the source of college funds (family, loan, scholarship). The answers will provide data for study of scholarship needs.

3. Plans for marriage and children — including the age at which a student plans to marry. This often relates to his occupational and college plans.

4. Economic aspirations — how much income does the student expect after graduation; what are his hopes for insurance, savings, securities, and real estate ownership? Such aspirations may relate to a student's economic gain in the future.

5. Plans for fulfilling military service requirements. Military service constitutes an obligation for most boys, and long-range educational and vocational goals may be delayed. For others the military is a potential career. Since the questions included choice of service branch and possible plans for a military career, the information obtained will permit an estimation of the part of the national talent pool each service might expect to obtain.

6. Occupational choices, decisions, and values. Here questions included specific occupation chosen; the occupation preferred; the grade in which the occupation was chosen; the number of different occupations considered; and the considerations, such as income, security, or interest in the work, that were important in making the decision.

10

How the Tests Were Given

> *Test booklets, answer sheets, stop watches, teachers with instructions manuals — these and other components of group testing faced nearly half a million students early in March of 1960. This chapter tells how the student provided hundreds of items of information about himself, his background, his knowledge, and his abilities.*
>
> *We describe the preparation needed to assure that each school and each student had the measuring tools ready and on hand; the work of the regional coordinators; the task that faced 18,000 teachers in giving a standardized test for which their students could do no special studying.*

At 9 A.M. on March 1, 1960, nearly all of the 225 students of the Riverside Indian School in Anadarko, Oklahoma, were seated in their homerooms. Today they were going to take tests for which no one had spent even a few minutes studying the night before. No preparation was possible for the TALENT tests, since they covered all school subjects — and some subjects not taught in school. Instead, it was the teachers who had prepared for the test. They had attended lectures and conferences, and had studied a book of instructions to be ready for this day.

On each teacher's desk were the test booklets on which the students were to work that morning. In addition, there were sheets on which the students would mark their answers, record forms, student identification cards, extra pencils, a stop-watch, and, of course, the instructions book. Written on each blackboard was:

DO NOT TURN OR OPEN YOUR TEST
BOOKLETS UNTIL TOLD TO DO SO.

The test booklets were passed out, then the sheets on which the boys and girls would indicate answers to test questions, and finally the student identification cards. Then each teacher read this statement:

"Starting today you will be taking part in a nation-wide study of high school talents. As a student in one of the high schools selected, you are part of a group that represents *all* high schools throughout the country. Only one in every twenty high schools will take part in this project.

"One of the things this study is trying to find out is what your best talents are. The tests will cover a wide range of topics. Some of the questions will be easy and some will be hard, but don't be discouraged by the hard ones, because no one is expected to be equally good in all areas. Just work as quickly and accurately as you can and try your very best.

"Our school will receive a summary of your test results. This information can be useful to your teachers, counselors, and advisors in helping you make plans for after high school."

Then, teachers read instructions on how the students were to record their answers on the specially constructed answer sheets. Since the answer sheets were devised so that they could be "read" by a machine, students were shown how to put down information about themselves by blacking in spaces to spell out their name and address, school code, grade, sex, and testing number (see Figures 6 and 7). Later on, the scoring machine would be able to "read" such information about each student while scoring his test.

For each question in the tests, the student was to choose an answer from among several which were offered, and then black in the appropriate space on the answer sheet (see Fig. 8 and Fig. 9).

FIGURE 6

Black Marks Give the Facts

This figure shows a portion of Project TALENT's Record Form Z, Side 1. On this form the student indicated his name, date of birth, age, and status in school.

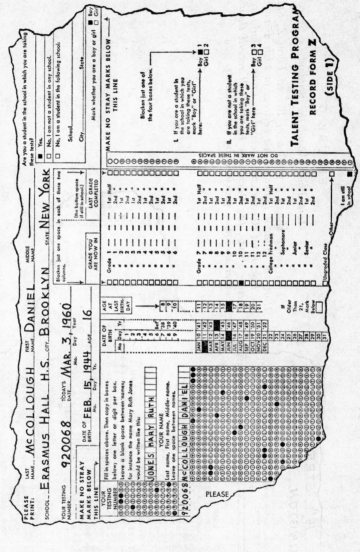

FIGURE 7

More Facts About the Student

This figure shows a portion of Record Form Z, Side 2.
Here the student indicated his address in such a way that
the Document Reader could record it. From similarly treated
answer sheets, the Document Reader will record thousands
of other responses provided by the students.

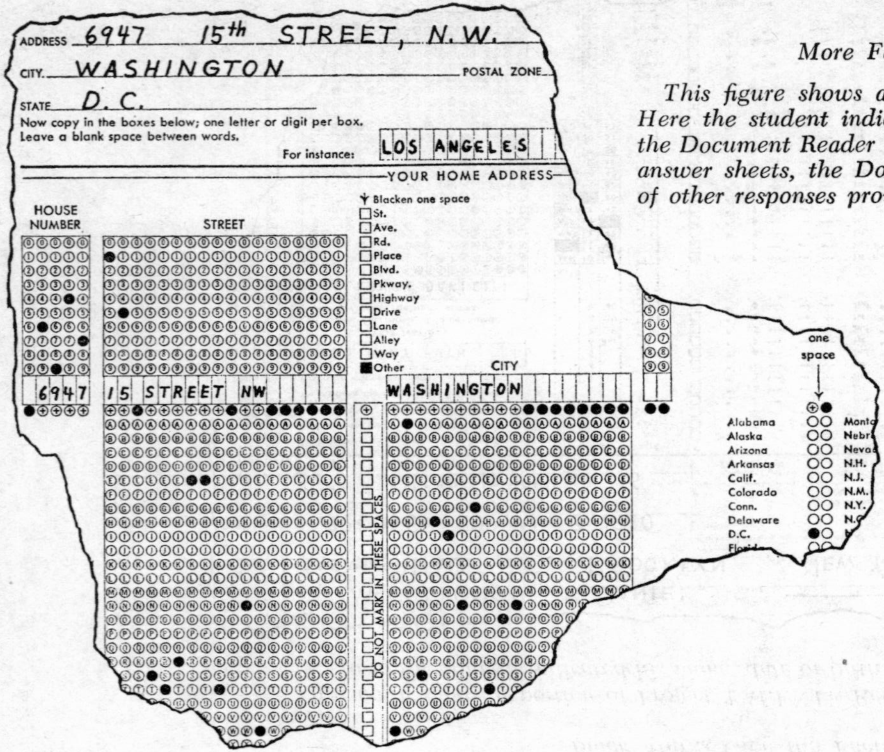

164

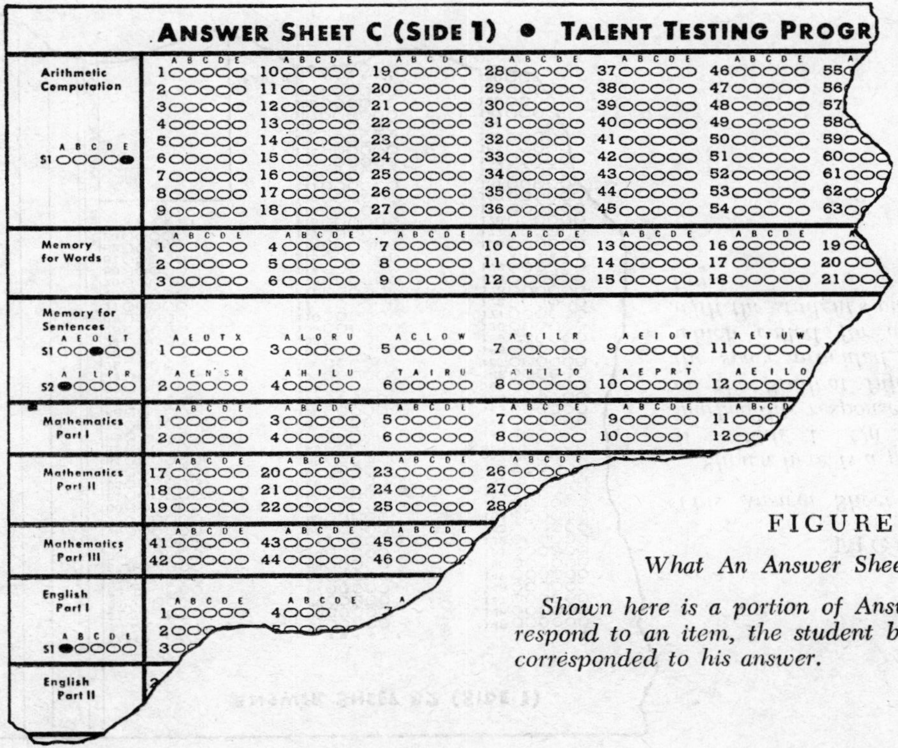

FIGURE 8

What An Answer Sheet Looks Like

Shown here is a portion of Answer Sheet C, Side 1. To respond to an item, the student blacked in the oval which corresponded to his answer.

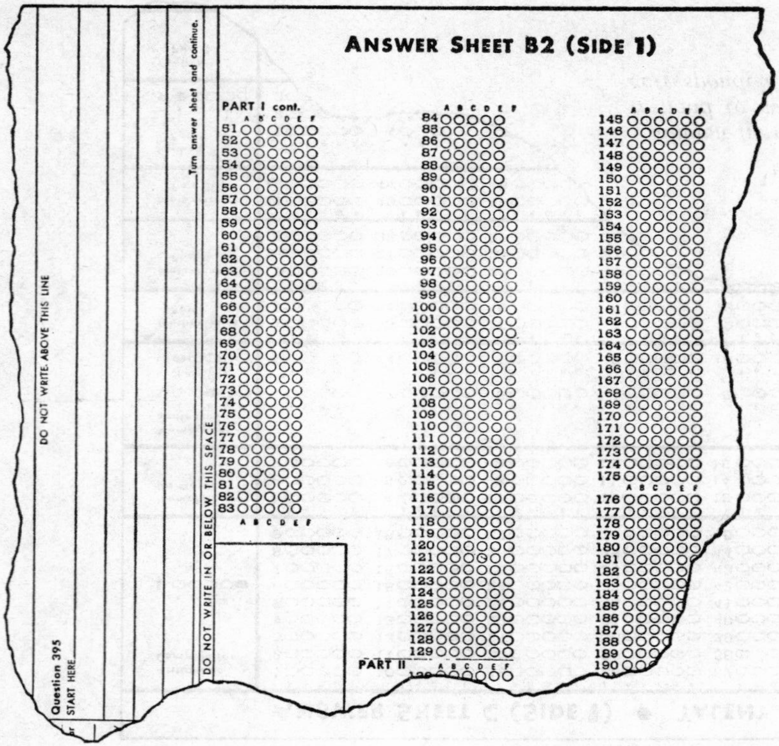

FIGURE 9

This Answer Sheet Required 80 Minutes

Shown here is a portion of Answer Sheet B 2, Side 1. On this sheet the student marked his responses to most of the items on the Student Information Blank. Note the space provided for Question No. 395, which called for a brief theme dealing with the student's view of his ideal occupation.

166

Now it was time to start the first test — the Information Test. Students opened their test booklets and began answering questions on literature, mechanics, mathematics, food, physics, music, electricity, biology, chemistry, home economics, geography, zoology, social studies, farming, space travel, sports — in fact, questions covering all kinds of general information students might have acquired in school or out. The test designers felt that this was a good test for students to start on, for all of them would feel at home in at least some of the fields. A boy might not know much about cooking or history, but he might be able to answer the questions about fishing or tools.

All that morning, that afternoon, the next morning, and the next afternoon the students of Riverside Indian School answered questions. At the end of the two days, each student had been asked nearly 2,000 questions — covering not only what he knew, but what he was interested in, what kind of a person he was, what his plans were. Each student probably answered more questions about himself than he ever had before. (See the schedule for the Final Battery, Table 4.)

The scene that took place at Riverside Indian School was repeated in 1,352 other schools from Madawaska, Maine, to Wailuku, Hawaii, in the spring of 1960. Schools and newspapers in many communities reported that attendance of pupils was noticeably higher on the days of testing than on comparable days in March of other years. Apparently, here was one testing experience American students did not wish to pass by.

2

To arrange with each of the 1,353 schools the details, schedules, and procedures for testing their students was a chore of some magnitude. It was managed for Project TALENT by 90 men and women known as regional coordinators. They had been selected by the TALENT staff from a list of outstanding educators and psychologists who could be expected to work well with school people. Many of them accepted the assignment knowing that it would have to be carried out on time outside their regular positions. Among them were heads of university departments (education, psychology, guidance); professors of

TABLE 4

Schedule for the Final TALENT Battery

This table lists the separate tests in the TALENT battery, showing the sequence in which they were taken and the time allowance for each test. It also notes the test booklets and answer sheets with which the students worked during the two-day testing period.

Test	Time (Minutes)*	Test Booklet Used	Answer Sheet Used
FIRST HALF-DAY			
Information Test — Part I	90		
BREAK	3		
Student Activities Inventory	20	A	A
Preferences	3		
Master Record Form	–		Z
SECOND HALF-DAY			
Interest Inventory	20		
Information Test — Part II	35		B
BREAK	3		
Student Information Blank	80	B	B1,
Paragraph Themes { On occupation	5		B
Paragraph Themes { On high school	5		B
THIRD HALF-DAY			
Memory for Sentences: Study	6		
Arithmetic Computation	9		
Memory for Words { Study	2	C1–X	
Memory for Words { Practice	2		
Memory for Words { Test	4		
Memory for Sentences: Test	10		
Mathematics { I Arithmetic Reasoning	12		
Mathematics { II Introductory Mathematics	24		
Mathematics { III Advanced Mathematics	14		
BREAK	3		C
English { I English Usage	10	C1	
English { II Effective Expression	10		
English { III Punctuation { a) Punctuation Marks	9		
English { III Punctuation { b) Sentence Structure	5		
English { IV Spelling	12		
English { V Capitalization	6		

Test	Time (Minutes)*	Test Booklet Used	Answer Sheet Used
FOURTH HALF-DAY			
Abstract Reasoning	11		
Mechanical Reasoning	11		
Disguised Words — Directions	1		
Disguised Words — Test	3		
Creativity — Directions	1		
Creativity — Test	20		
Clerical Checking	3		
Visualization in Two Dimensions	4	C2	C
BREAK	3		
Reading Comprehension	30		
Visualization in Three Dimensions	9		
Word Functions in Sentences — Directions	2½		
Word Functions in Sentences — Test	15		
Table Reading	3		
Object Inspection	3		

* Times given are for actual tests (not for directions, etc.) unless otherwise specified.

education and psychology; a dean of a graduate school; a director of research for a public school system; a state supervisor of guidance; a dean of a university school of education; an assistant superintendent of schools; a director of a student counseling bureau; a university examiner; a director of student personnel in a university. Some of the regional coordinators were in private practice; others had retired. One link among them was their interest in young people — in their education, guidance, and vocational success.

The regional coordinators made trips to each of the schools chosen for the study to tell the story of Project TALENT to the school staff — and later to help in preparing teachers for giving the tests.

The responsibility for deciding to give the tests was that of the superintendents and principals. Occasionally, Board of Education members were brought in to consider the Project. Finally, the cooperation of more than 18,000 teachers had to be obtained to bring the work of the Project to its first culmination point.

The achievement of the regional coordinators in dealing with the thousands of school people was spectacular, considering that even getting an appointment with one of them was sometimes challenging. A coordinator reported: "One school on my list didn't have a phone. The principal didn't have a phone in his house, either." Getting to the school was often more challenging. One coordinator recalled: "Some of my travel was done at the time when heavy winter snows made the mountain roads impassable. I had to buy chains to reach one town." Another reported: "I located the town on the map and found a road that cut out quite a bit of the distance. My car got mired down in the mud. . . . I ended up driving 200 miles around to get to a place that was only 25 miles away."

Reports from regional coordinators also describe the reception they received at the schools:

> ". . . there's eagerness to participate in a project of national scope and significance. Some principals hardly let me finish my spiel before they accepted. Although I always explained that the school was selected at random, many people seemed to give participation in the project some honorific value . . ."

> ". . . principals of two schools were suspicious of me — thinking that their schools had been selected because of their poverty, both instructionally and economically. . . . But I've encountered no real hostility."

> ". . . the cooperation of the schools has been most gratifying. Every school gave the impression that they were delighted at the opportunity to participate."

These are, of course, impressionistic accounts. They do, however, suggest that schoolmen were eager to take part in the project. This was true in spite of the fact that in some schools there was the feeling of "too much testing." In some high schools, a half-dozen standardized tests had been scheduled for the school year and teachers had been known to complain that they were doing more testing than teaching. There seemed to be several reasons for the cooperation accorded Project TALENT. Counselors and guidance directors were responsive because they understood that the study would help in their own guidance programs. Then, too, many school people felt that participation was a patriotic service. They took part not so much because of what they would get out of the study, but because of its ultimate contribution to the nation. In addition, a few of the schools had had little opportunity to do any testing before because of lack of funds, physical facilities, and staff. Project TALENT presented them with an opportunity for a new experience in evaluation.

3

No matter how much testing experience individual schools had or did not have, Project TALENT still had to train more than 18,000 teachers to give all the tests in the same way.

Why was this training necessary? Are not classroom teachers experts in test-giving? The answer is that there is a difference between the techniques of giving a test on a subject regularly taught in a classroom and those of administering standardized tests. Teachers give tests regularly as part of their course work to check on how well their instruction is faring; to assess the progress students are making; and to discover weak spots in the students' mastery of facts or skills. Very often the questions in teacher-made tests review the material which has been taught the previous week or month. In all cases, teacher-made tests are designed to advance the teacher's plans of instruction. It may be part of the teacher's plan to allow individual pupils as much time as each one needs; and even to let pupils grade the tests themselves as part of their learning tasks.

A standardized test, however, is constructed so that the questions will sample specific knowledge, traits, interests, or other facets of the individual. A standardized test is always administered the same way to all students who take it. The directions for the test are prescribed in a manual and are read to the students. Generally there is a time limit for a standardized test — and it must be adhered to carefully. If one student were allowed a few more minutes than the established time he would have an advantage over other students. In scoring the test, there is no guesswork about whether the answer is right or wrong. The rules and standards for correct answers are set up beforehand.

When a test is developed carefully, given correctly, and scored accurately and impartially, it is possible to say with some confidence that we have measured accurately some part of the person tested. Furthermore, if someone else administered the same test to another group of students at a later time and if the directions were followed precisely, the score of any student could be compared with the scores of the group which was first tested, and his score evaluated. Therefore, to make a score on a standardized test meaningful, teachers giving the tests must be familiar with, and follow meticulously, the procedures of standardized test administration.

In some schools counselors with considerable training and experience in giving standardized tests were available to help teachers give the TALENT battery. In other schools, there were limited or no counseling facilities and teachers had never given standardized tests before. Thus, the amount of teacher training necessary varied from school to school. In some cases, the regional coordinators briefed the counselors, who in turn went over the details of testing with the teaching staff. In other cases, the regional coordinators personally went over every detail of the two-day testing program with the teachers to be sure that procedures were thoroughly understood.

When the test materials arrived at a school, they became the responsibility of one person — generally the school principal or head counselor. It was his job to receive the materials and distribute them on the testing days; to gather up the materials at the end of each half-day; to organize the answer sheets for shipment to the scoring center; and, of course, to monitor the testing. In all, there were 21 different items used in conducting the tests — ranging from the test booklets and answer sheets to teachers' guides, aids to students in filling out certain answer sheets, school questionnaires, mailing labels, and so on. Each school also received a manual on school arrangements, for use by the individual responsible for the testing. An important part of his assignment was to see that the test materials were sorted and counted out for each homeroom. This was no small task, particularly in a large school which had received a truckload of test supplies.

All the effort that went into training the teachers and into careful distribution of the test materials was for one purpose — to insure that every student had the same opportunity to do well on the tests.

Two methods of giving the tests were used. The more common was for each homeroom teacher to give the tests to his students.

However, in a number of schools the directions were read to all students at once by one person through the public address system. In such cases there was only one timekeeper — and thus no variation in timing for the tests within the school. The teachers acted as proctors in each room. Although a failure or two in public address systems caused some difficulty, the method appeared to be efficient.

The tests were given either on two full school days or on four half-days. When they were completed, the answer sheets were sorted, arranged, and shipped to Project TALENT by each school for the next step — scoring and processing.

11 Analyzing the Data

We take a look at the electronic computers and other machines which help the present-day investigator. We follow one student's answer sheets to see how investigator and machine record and analyze his scores.

Next we tell why four per cent of the replies were processed first and how this partial analysis serves the need of the total study.

We describe the means for storing nearly a billion items of information for later research — research which will continue into the next two decades. Finally, we present a brief introduction to some of the methods — statistical and other — which will be used in analyzing and interpreting the facts obtained.

The testing was over! Almost half a million students had filled out more than two million answer sheets. These had been shipped to our processing center and there they were — some ten tons of paper. How does one go about handling ten tons of answer sheets? The solution lay in a single word — "automation." If astonishing progress had not been made in the past few years in the technology of processing and scoring answer sheets by machine, Project TALENT would have been impossible.

From the beginning the project was planned in such a way that automatic data-processing capabilities could be utilized throughout. Answer sheets for tests were designed so that they could be scored by the Iowa Electronic Test Scoring Machine; student questionnaires were set up so that responses could be punched by the Iowa Document Reader. These machines represent vast advances in automatic scoring. Automatic scoring has come a long way since 1937, the year that IBM came out with the first electrical scoring machine. Operation of that machine depended on the fact that carbon conducts electricity. Since pencil "lead" is made of graphite, a form of carbon, it is possible to conduct electricity through a pencil mark on a test answer sheet, thus closing an electrical circuit and causing a point to be added to the test score. The early IBM machines based on this principle took the scoring of objective tests out of the horse-and-buggy age. And a new age of scoring arrived in 1955, when the Iowa Electronic Test Scoring Machine went into operation.

This machine uses photoelectric cells (the same basic components that cause a door with an "electric eye" to open automatically when someone approaches). The answer sheet is scanned by an infra-red beam, and the photoelectric cell senses which of several possible answers for an item is the one which has been marked. The machine counts the number of "right" responses. Even if the student has ignored the instructions to mark only one answer for each item, or has failed to erase an answer thoroughly when he changed his mind, the machine can still cope with the situation. It does this by determining which of several marks is the darkest one. The darkest mark is assumed to indicate the student's answer, the lighter marks presumably being incomplete erasures. If two or more responses are equally dark, the machine treats the item as if it had been omitted.

The speed at which the machine works represents a vast improvement, too, over earlier machines. Answer sheets are scored at the rate of more than 5,000 per hour. As many as 13 independent scores can be obtained from each answer sheet, plus a number of composites, each representing a weighted sum of several of these 13 scores. Thus nearly 100,000 scores can be obtained in an hour. Compare this with the top rate of 800 scores an hour on any earlier machine! Furthermore, for each answer sheet, the Iowa Test Scoring Machine punches an IBM card on which all the student's scores are recorded.

Still a newer development is the Iowa Document Reader. This is not another scoring machine; its function is entirely different. Many items in our test battery are not designed to contribute toward a "score"; instead, they constitute independent items of information. Consider, for example, the answers to the questions in our Student Information Blank. The individual answers have to be preserved. Eventually, of course, selected sub-sets of these items will be combined in a designated way to answer future research questions, but the items have to be kept separate so that many ways of combining them can be tried if it seems desirable. There is also Record Form Z, which gives the student's name, address, date of birth, grade, and other information. All these items of information must be recorded individually. The Iowa Document Reader takes care of these needs by making it possible to transfer each individual response from the answer sheet or record form directly to punched cards. Like the Iowa Scoring Machine, the Document Reader uses photoelectric cells to "read" the responses — in other words, to sense which response position is darkest for each question. The student's responses to as many as 140 separate items can be punched simultaneously on a single card.

2

Let's see now what happened to one typical student's answer sheets.

Consider Johnny Dover, a sophomore at Centerville High School. Suppose that this hypothetical youngster, Johnny, has been told that his testing number is 674,425. The code for Centerville High is F–896. (To preserve the anonymity of students and schools and to facilitate the data processing and analysis, each student was identified by a six-digit number; the school code consisted of a letter followed by three digits. Each school was told its own code, but not the code of other schools.) Johnny has worked carefully on the tests and has filled out his answer sheets properly, putting his testing number on each one of them.

When Johnny's teacher collected the answer sheets, they were taken to a central room to which all the other teachers had brought the answer sheets for their classes. Here, under the supervision of, say, Mr. Brown, the guidance counselor designated by the principal to serve as local coordinator of the Project TALENT testing, the answer sheets were packed and shipped to the Measurement Research Center, in Iowa City. There they were stored for a few weeks in a room in which a constant temperature of 68° F and a humidity level of 50% were maintained to "condition" them for the Scoring Machine or the Document Reader.

The answer sheets were now ready for scoring. Let's follow Johnny's *Answer Sheet C* to see what happened to it.

Johnny's answer sheet went through the Scoring Machine twice. The machine determined his scores and punched them on two IBM cards. Then followed a complex series of steps in which man and machine worked together to assure that no slip-ups had taken place; that the scores which the machine punched on Johnny's card were really Johnny's; and that they were the scores he had actually made on the test. This checking procedure is so elaborate that the likelihood that any substantial errors in Johnny's scores will get through undetected is very slight.

The processing of *Answer Sheet A* was similar to that described for *Answer Sheet C*. The other three sheets — B1, B2, and Z — went through the Document Reader. Again, the cards were "edited" to locate and correct possible errors and slip-ups.

Next, we proceeded to print the reports to be sent to the schools. On these reports appeared both the raw scores and the percentile scores of each student in the school. A section of the report for Grade 10 in Centerville High School is shown in Table 5. Johnny's scores appear on the list. His raw score on Arithmetic Computation, for instance, is 51, which puts him at the 97th percentile for Grade 10. (Johnny is good at arithmetic.)

The two answer sheets that were put through the Scoring Machine (A and C) yielded 26 scores apiece, plus eight composites — a total of 60 scores. Of these, the scores for the 37 tests shown in Table 6 were sent to the schools. The remaining scores were not reported, since they were for tests of an experimental character or of such a nature that they would have little utility for the schools. The 60 scores obtained on the scoring machine are listed in the Appendix, Section E.

3

The reports to the schools included not only the raw scores on 37 tests, but also the corresponding percentiles.[1] These were

[1] A percentile is a numerical value which indicates how someone stands on a test or other variable in comparison with a specified group. The 80th percentile, for example, is the raw score point below which 80% of the individuals in the basic group score and above which the remaining 20% score. Thus a percentile can have any value between 0 and 100.

Separate percentile tables were obtained for each grade. For four of the

TABLE 5

Report to the Schools

Shown here is a portion of the report that was sent to Centerville High School (the name is obviously fictitious). It gives the scores which Centerville students made on the TALENT tests. Johnny Dover's scores, as well as those of other students, are

CENTERVILLE		F896		GRADE	10		STANDARD				
		211 MMS RS PR	212 MMW RS PR	220 DSW RS PR	231 SPL RS PR	232 CAP RS PR	233 PNC RS PR	234 USG RS PR	235 EXP RS PR	230 ENG RS PR	240 WDF RS PR
TEST NO.	NAME										
674425	J B Dover	9 / 49	16 / 83	25 / 94	12 / 86	32 / 87	23 / 90	19 / 81	11 / 90	97 / 93	14 / 78
674426	T E Dow	14 / 95	8 / 34	17 / 69	6 / 19	29 / 36	14 / 29	12 / 11	7 / 29	68 / 20	10 / 61
674427	N J Dugan	8 / 37	11 / 58	12 / 44	10 / 66	31 / 69	16 / 43	18 / 70	9 / 58	84 / 63	11 / 66
674428	S I Dunbarto	13 / 90	19 / 92	18 / 73	12 / 86	32 / 87	19 / 66	20 / 89	7 / 29	90 / 79	19 / 94
674429	L N Edgerton	11 / 73	22 / 97	28 / 98	9 / 55	29 / 36	14 / 29	18 / 70	9 / 58	79 / 46	13 / 66

preliminary norms obtained on the basis of a four per cent sub-sample of the entire group of schools in which testing had taken place (except the schools whose answer sheets were not received in time for inclusion).

Why were the percentiles based on a four per cent sample, rather than on the entire set of available data? The answer is that even with modern high-speed digital electronic computers available, data processing still hasn't reached the speed of light!

Information Test scales there are separate tables for boys and girls in each grade. The four scales given this special treatment were: Aeronautics and Space, Electricity and Electronics, Mechanics, and Home Economics. Having separate sets of norms for boys and girls seemed appropriate in the cases of these four scales because they were in areas in which boys and girls customarily receive different training.

given as "raw scores," and also in percentiles. School guidance staff members know how to interpret these figures. Nevertheless, Project TALENT provided the schools with a technical manual designed to help school people make the most effective use of the scores.

250	260	270	281	282	290	311	312	320	333	340	410	420	430	440
RDG	CRE	MCR	VS2	VS3	ABS	ARR	MA9	SUM	ADV	TOT	ARC	TBL	CLR	OBJ
RS	RS	RS	RS	RS	RS	RS	RS	RS	RS	RS	RS	RS	RS	RS
PR	PR	PR	PR	PR	PR	PR	PR	PR	PR	PR	PR	PR	PR	PR
39	10	9	18	13	12	8	18	26	5	31	51	25	69	40
82	70	42	82	92	87	55	95	86	88	88	97	97	98	99
29	11	10	14	6	7	8	5	13	1	14	38	17	0	38
52	78	50	56	27	30	55	13	30	19	24	75	91	10	98
20	12	8	14	8	8	7	12	19	4	23	33	5	29	31
26	84	33	56	49	41	45	72	62	77	67	61	27	64	90
34	10	7	12	14	13	9	16	25	4	29	43	21	42	25
68	70	25	42	96	94	64	90	84	77	84	86	95	85	71
37	13	8	11	11	11	8	8	16	1	17	38	34	34	36
77	88	33	36	78	76	55	39	46	19	39	75	98	74	96

TABLE 6

*Code Designation of Tests Reported to the Schools**

CODE		TEST
102	VOC	Information — Vocabulary
103	LIT	Literature
104	MUS	Music
105	SST	Social Studies
106	MAT	Mathematics
107	PHY	Physical Science
108	BIO	Biological Science
110	AER	Aeronautics and Space
111	ELE	Electricity and Electronics
112	MEC	Mechanics
114	HEC	Home Economics
190	INF	Information — Total
211	MMS	Memory for Sentences
212	MMW	Memory for Words
220	DSW	Disguised Words
231	SPL	English — Spelling
232	CAP	Capitalization
233	PNC	Punctuation
234	USG	English Usage
235	EXP	Effective Expression
230	ENG	English — Total
240	WDF	Word Functions in Sentences
250	RDG	Reading Comprehension
260	CRE	Creativity
270	MCR	Mechanical Reasoning
281	VS2	Visualization in Two Dimensions
282	VS3	Visualization in Three Dimensions
290	ABS	Abstract Reasoning
311	ARR	Mathematics I — Arithmetic Reasoning
312	MA9	Mathematics II — Introductory
320	SUM	Mathematics I + II
333	ADV	Mathematics III — Advanced
340	TOT	Mathematics — Total (I + II + III)
410	ARC	Arithmetic Computation
420	TBL	Table Reading
430	CLR	Clerical Checking
440	OBJ	Object Inspection

* This table lists 37 scores (together with their 3-digit code numbers and their 3-letter designations). These 37 scores are the ones that Project TALENT reported to the schools, for use in counseling and for other educational purposes.

It takes time to transfer the data from cards to magnetic tape — an essential step in order to be able to utilize the high-speed operation of the computer. Hence, as an expedient, preliminary norms, based on four per cent of the sample, were obtained. The six-digit student testing numbers made it easy to make this "sample of a sample" representative of the available cases. All answer sheets were selected that had a testing number with 00, 25, 50, or 75 as the last two digits. These four per cent included over 12,000 students, from over 1000 schools. By most standards, this is a very respectable number of cases on which to base test norms.

Nevertheless, it is well to bear in mind that the norms thus obtained are tentative and subject to revision. Eventually, we want national norms based on a truly national, truly representative sample. Our four per cent sample is almost that, but not quite. It falls short chiefly because the answer sheets were not received from some of the schools in time for inclusion.[2] Not all of the schools had even completed their testing by the cut-off date. In round numbers, about 80 per cent of the answer sheets had been received by then. We hope these cases are reasonably representative of the full sample — in other words that the missing 20% does not differ substantially in any important respect from the 80% that were on hand. But we have no real basis for *asserting* that this is the case. Hence, the stress on "tentative," and "subject to revision."

Because of these limitations, school counselors were urged to use caution in interpreting the scores. Also, until the students who took the tests go to college, or work at a job, it can only be *inferred* that a certain score on any of the tests is likely to predict future success in a particular field. Nevertheless, since the kinds of tests included in the battery were carefully selected and the tests themselves carefully constructed, the schools found the results helpful supplements to other available information, in the occupational and educational guidance of students. To help them make the best use of the results, schools that participated in the project were sent a manual containing the preliminary norms together with suggestions on the use and interpretation of test scores of these types.

[2] The four per cent sample was selected from answer sheets received by May 7, 1960.

In addition to its major purpose, which was to provide a basis for tentative norms, the four per cent sample had other uses. Besides the 60 scores obtained on the Scoring Machine for all students in the Project, 53 additional scores[3] were obtained for the students in the four per cent sample. They were needed primarily for research use in connection with certain technical problems.

4

Since most of the data analysis lies in the future, the means for storing the information and for having it in ready reserve for processing are worth describing at this point.

As we have already noted, the basic data have been transferred to punched cards, primarily by the Scoring Machine and the Document Reader. Next, the data will be put on electromagnetic tape (often called magnetic tape) to store it compactly and to permit subsequent processing on digital electronic computers.

Most of the data processing will be done on the giant computer at the University of Pittsburgh. This machine is an "IBM–7070." The 7070 is still a comparatively new machine — new even in a field where technological progress is so rapid that yesterday's eighth wonder of the world is today's commonplace and tomorrow's obsolescent relic. The 7070 is a solid-state (transistorized), fully "buffered," high-speed, general-purpose decimal computer that can "remember" as many as 99,900 digits. The memory is in the form of "core storage." The computer uses high-density tape, it has two channels, and it can run as many as six reels at a time. In addition to the tape input and output, it also has card input (a high-speed card reader), card output, and a printer.

Another feature of the 7070 is "automatic priority processing." This feature makes the computer capable of running two or more independent programs at the same time. This capability for unrelated simultaneous activities can be put to practical use on Project TALENT. For example, at the same time that the cards are being converted to magnetic tape they can be alphabetized and edited.

Unlike the information punched in cards, the information now converted to magnetic tape is not represented by visible holes,

3 The additional 53 scores are shown in the Appendix, Section E.

but by invisible patterns of magnetized spots. Such a record is extremely compact. A 2400-foot reel of half-inch tape, which has a diameter of only 10½ inches, can contain about 15 million individual characters. Each character is either a letter of the alphabet, one of the 10 digits, or a special symbol. To give some idea of the speed with which the 7070 can handle these tapes, a reel containing about 15 million characters can be run through the machine in less than 10 minutes.

To see how this storage of information in a manner suitable for machine processing works, consider *Item 305* of the Student Information Blank, which reads as follows:

Have you taken, or do you expect to take, the National Merit Scholarship Tests?

A. No, I have not taken, nor do I expect to take these tests.
B. Yes, I expect to take these tests.
C. Yes, I have taken these tests.

Suppose that a student marks Answer B, indicating that he expects to take the National Merit Scholarship Tests. His response would appear on the answer sheet as shown in Figure 10. Figure 11 shows how this response would appear in the card punched on the Document Reader. These diagrams are the actual size. Figure 12 shows a greatly magnified representation of the pattern of magnetized spots that would appear on the electromagnetic tape to represent response B. There are 556 such characters per inch on the tape.

Compactness of storage and speed of processing have been mentioned as advantages of magnetic tape. A third advantage is its flexibility. It will be necessary to bring the tape up to date after the one-year, five-year, ten-year, and twenty-year follow-ups. This can be achieved automatically if the machine is "programmed" to accomplish this — that is, if the machine is given appropriate instructions in "machine language."

The use of high-speed computers makes it possible to incorporate into the data analysis a very large number of items of information about each individual — far more than one could even begin to consider if this kind of equipment were not available. The results, therefore, can provide a view of the individual student in depth, not just a flat two-dimensional picture lacking perspective.

FIGURE 10

How the Student Marked His Answer

This is a section of Answer Sheet B–2, showing how responses are marked for Student Information Blank Item 305 and adjacent items.

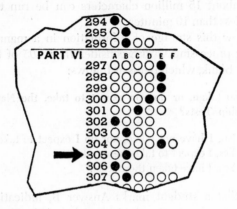

FIGURE 11

From Answer Sheet to IBM Card

Section of an IBM card showing responses punched for Student Information Blank Item 305 and adjacent items. The black rectangles represent punched holes.

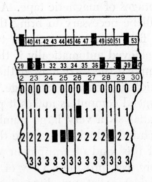

FIGURE 12

From IBM Card to Tape

A small segment of tape is shown about double its actual width and tremendously elongated. The black marks represent magnetic spots.

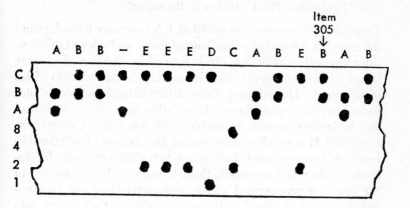

Item
305
↓

5

After transferring the basic data from 5,000,000 punched cards to magnetic tape and identifying and eliminating invalid scores, we shall be ready for the data analysis itself. Many studies lie ahead. What will be our procedure?

Back in Chapter 2 we indicated some of the questions we hope to answer on the basis of the analysis of Project TALENT data. To be specific, let's focus on this question: "Is the high school which spends more money for its pupils more efficient in developing men and women who are successful in developing and utilizing their talents?" For purposes of the present discussion, let's narrow the problem to just one aspect — a very important aspect, though: "Are high school graduates who have aptitude for college work more likely to go to college if their high school has a high per capita expenditure than if its per capita expenditure is low?"

Before we can get the answer to this question, we have to define college aptitude. Let's tentatively define it for our purposes as a high score on a composite of the following five tests:

1. Information (total score)
2. English (total score)
3. Reading Comprehension
4. Abstract Reasoning
5. Mathematics, Part I (Arithmetic Reasoning)

To get at the answer to our question, it is necessary to understand the complex interrelationship among many variables. Let's consider three: the student's aptitude for college, the fact of whether he goes to college or not, and the per capita expenditures of his high school. Determining these interrelationships necessitates some statistical procedures. Correlation is a major statistical tool in finding answers to problems of this sort. A correlation coefficient is a number representing the degree of relationship between two measures (scores on two different tests, for instance). As a first approach, then, toward getting an answer to the question propounded above, intercorrelations can be computed among students' aptitude for college, their entry into college, and their high schools' per capita expenditure rate. (Considerable further analysis of the resultant values will of course be necessary before we can hope to have anything approaching a definitive answer to the question propounded.)

Correlation coefficients can be helpful in answering other sorts of questions, too. For instance, we can compute the relationship that may exist between —

a. Class size and amount of subject matter learned, thus obtaining a clue as to whether small classes are more effective than large ones, as some people have claimed.

b. Size of school and dropout rate, thus, perhaps, getting an inkling as to the extent to which school size may prove to be related to important outcomes of the educational effort.

c. Average income of parents and percentage of high school graduates entering college, thus getting evidence of the extent to which family income is related to a student's enrollment in college.

d. Distance from nearest college and percentage of students

from any designated community enrolling as freshmen, thus obtaining a clue on the need for community colleges.

Using still another statistical method, with the help of electronic computers, we can correlate one measure with another while, at the same time, the effect of other measures can be ruled out — or, in other words, the influence of these other measures can be "held constant."

For example, we can study the relationship between —

a. Size of class and per cent of the school's graduates who enter college (holding constant the average income of the parents, nearness to a college, rural-urban nature of the school's location, size of the school).

b. Average per-pupil expenditure and average reading comprehension score of the students (holding constant size of the school, rural-urban factor, average income of parents, occupation of the father).

We can compute such "partial correlation coefficients," holding constant up to 90 or 100 other measures. This will help us to isolate unique relationships between pairs of measures.

Other tools of the statistician will also have roles in the fact-finding process — tools with such resounding names as "multiple regression analysis," "analysis of variance," "analysis of covariance"; tools with deceptively simple-sounding names like "factor analysis"; and tools with odd-sounding names like "chi-square." All these tools will be useful to us in leading up to sound answers to questions of interest to parents, teachers, and others with an interest in education. Computing simple averages (or means) will also provide us with a wealth of facts about youth and their schools. Let's look at one set of facts, concerning reading ability, that we hope to obtain at one stage of the data analysis. We shall determine, for instance, the average reading comprehension score for:

1. The entire group of twelfth-graders.
2. Twelfth-graders in an academic curriculum in high school.
3. Twelfth-graders who plan to go to college.
4. Twelfth-graders who actually go to college.
5. Twelfth-graders who go to college and who plan to become scientists.

Reading is an important ability, and the facts indicated above will be useful to teachers, counselors, and students. For instance, a student who plans to go to college will be under a handicap if his reading ability is substantially below that of most of his college classmates, even if he is about average in comparison with high school seniors in general. Thus, these sets of "norms" for reading comprehension will tell how a given student stands in relation to various special groups with which it is appropriate to compare him.

Such studies can be made only because the sample is sufficiently large, thus making it possible to identify reasonable numbers of students with highly superior abilities, students with plans to go into occupations for which few people can qualify (e.g., nuclear physicist), and students with unusual combinations of traits and unusual interests. In other words, extremes as well as means can be studied.

But more than that, the Project is not limited to studying secondary school students. Because an entire age group — all 15 year-olds whether in secondary school or not — was sampled, it will be possible to draw some inferences in regard to this much broader and more general base — which, unlike the sample of high school students, is a random sampling of "people-in-general."

In addition, special studies will be done of *schools*. We will want to find out, for instance, the percentage of schools offering instruction in French; in Russian; in physics; and the percentage offering four years of mathematics. These data will be of interest in themselves, and some of them will be of even greater interest when considered in conjunction with other data. For instance, in high schools offering four years of mathematics, what proportion of those students who, on the basis of their scores on Part II of our mathematics test have the ability to do well in advanced mathematics, neglect to take any mathematics beyond Grade 9? And in schools that offer no college-preparatory mathematics beyond, say, the ninth grade, what percentage of the students could profit from such instruction if it were offered?

The number of questions of this type that can be asked (and answered) about the schools is almost infinite, but here are two more for illustration:

1. What proportion of the high schools have at least 100 seniors?

2. What percentage of high schools with fewer than 100 seniors offer as full programs as the typical high school that has more than 100 seniors? (Note in this connection that James B. Conant, in his report on "The American High School Today," has suggested 100 seniors as the division point above which high schools can generally offer a varied curriculum and below which they cannot, except at much greater cost per capita.)

With 1,353 schools being tested, and with procedures for weighting the schools so as to reconstruct the "population" of secondary schools in the United States as a whole, it will be possible to find out what typical schools are like, how schools differ, and how the characteristics in which they differ are related to their success in educating young America. Perhaps most important of all, the results may point to ways in which some schools can improve their offerings, policies, and practices.

6

One problem which has implications for many aspects of the project is that of follow-up. Students are already being asked to report on their activities — educational and employment — one year after graduation. Other follow-ups will be made five, ten, and twenty years after graduation from high school. The prospects of getting cooperation from the students are good. Naturally, the follow-up will become progressively more difficult over the years, as members of the group change their addresses and forget to notify the Project TALENT Office, change their names, or for some other reason become difficult to locate, or disinclined to report their activities.

One device which we hope will recover some of these lost cases is to reverse the follow-up procedure. The reverse procedure, which is here designated the "follow-back procedure," involves finding out the names and approximate ages of the members of any specified group which is of particular interest 10 or 20 years from now, finding out which members of the group are of the right age to have been tested in Project TALENT, and then acting on the assumption that approximately 5% of these people were in Project TALENT. (This is not an unreasonable assumption, since approximately 5% of today's high school students *are* included in the Project.)

Let's see how this follow-back procedure would work in a specific instance. Suppose that twenty years from now there is an interest in studying the backgrounds that are predictive of literary success, for instance of persons who have become outstanding authors and journalists. Lists could be searched, and the names of such persons who are in the right age range could be extracted. IBM cards could be punched for these persons, showing their name, date of birth, sex, and other appropriate identifying information. The computer would then be set up to "search the file" for these names. Presumably about 5% of them would be located. The Student Activities Inventory scores, responses on the Student Information Blank and Interest Inventory, test scores, and other relevant data for these individuals could then be studied intensively and compared with the corresponding data for the total group in the study or for any segment of it. This would provide information on what these people were like when they were in high school, what backgrounds they had, and in what respects, if any, they differed from their contemporaries.

7

We have discussed briefly our expectations of finding out some important things about high school boys and girls, about their futures, and about their schools and the roles these schools play in their lives. One other important area we expect to study has perhaps been implied but not stated explicitly; that area is the tests themselves. The long-term follow-up on a huge group of students will provide an unprecedented opportunity for adding to the store of knowledge concerning how effective various kinds of tests are in predicting success in different academic and vocational areas. This is the problem of "test validation." Ways of selecting and combining test scores to get the best predictions will be determined. Let's consider a specific example — accountants. There are several tests in the battery that are believed to be useful in predicting success in an accounting career. In the course of our follow-up, we can not only check up on how successful individual tests are (the Arithmetic Reasoning Test, for instance), but also find out what weighted combination of tests will give the best prediction of whether a student eventually becomes a successful certified public accountant.

12

The

Questionnaires: Surveying

School Characteristics

In the previous chapters we dealt with measuring devices designed to find out some about people. We described how the data about the young people would be analyzed. Now we come to a point in our study where we are concerned primarily with educational institutions.

This chapter, then, takes up the first of three questionnaires designed to survey schools and school programs. The General School Characteristics Questionnaire sought facts about school policies, practices, teaching staff, students, financial support and expenditures, community relations, and the school leadership.

The chapter indicates how the data gathered by this questionnaire can be used to construct pictures of schools of all types. We then sketch in three types of schools and indicate how the information we have gathered about can will help us understand the values and influences behind student progress.

12

The Questionnaires: Surveying School Characteristics

In the previous chapters we dealt with measuring devices designed to find out more about people. We also described how the data about the young people would be analyzed. Now we come to a point in our story where we are concerned primarily with educational institutions.

This chapter, then, takes up the first of three questionnaires developed to survey schools and school programs. The General School Characteristics Questionnaire sought facts about school policies, practices, plant, teaching staff, students, financial support and expenditures, community relations, and the school leadership.

The chapter indicates how the data gathered by this questionnaire can be used to construct pictures of schools of all types. We then sketch in three types of schools and indicate how the information we have gathered about each will help us understand the causes and influences behind student progress.

Children are developed through many influences, not the least of which are the schools they attend. To understand more fully the background and abilities of the children themselves, it was necessary to learn about their schools. To do this we developed a new instrument, the General School Characteristics Questionnaire.

This questionnaire was designed to provide information about those characteristics of the school which might make a difference in the education of its students as compared with those of other schools. Hence, at about the time the students were taking the Project TALENT tests, an administrator in each school, usually the principal, filled out the General School Characteristics Questionnaire.

To what use will this information be put? Primarily it will serve as a backdrop against which to interpret student data. For example, suppose we decide to study the achievement test scores for seniors who plan to be scientists. Many school characteristics could affect these scores — for instance, the number and types of science and math courses offered by the school. Other factors could be important and would have to be examined before valid conclusions could be drawn. Such factors might include size of school, size of classes, percentage of male teachers, number of grades in the school, years of teaching experience of staff, guidance facilities, acceleration-promotion policies — to name only a few characteristics which might make a difference in the development of future scientists. It might be that only a few, or perhaps none, of these factors would have any bearing on the achievement test scores of seniors planning to be scientists. The important thing is that the availability of such information about the schools will make it possible to study and measure the relationship of such factors to the abilities, achievements, ambitions, and later, the productivity of students.

The example above is only one of many uses to which data obtained by the General School Characteristics Questionnaire can be put. Broadly speaking, we are interested in studying the long-range effects of various school policies and practices on career choices of students and their later satisfactions and successes.

In addition, we are interested in the characteristics of the nation's schools themselves. For example: How old is the average school building? How large is the average class in city schools, in country schools, in the North, in the South? What percentage of the high schools offer courses in Russian? How many schools have science labs? Through its large and representative sample of the nation's high schools, Project TALENT has worked toward providing the most complete information on these and other topics that has ever been available.

2

From the beginning, the General School Characteristics Questionnaire seemed destined to be of great length. As we began to review educational research and to develop the questions, their number grew and grew. When an early draft of the lengthy questionnaire was submitted to the advisory panel charged with responsibility for defining appropriate educational issues for study, panel members responded with an even longer list of questions. These included virtually all of the characteristics of a school which might influence educational achievement and decisions — such items as the culture of the school and community, physical features of the school and community, school policies and practices, and course offerings. At each of the later meetings of the panel, additional areas for inclusion in the school characteristics questionnaire were proposed. But, remembering the principal — his crowded work schedule, the limits on his time and patience — we weighed each question carefully, pruned those least essential, and finally devised a trial questionnaire which was sent to seven high school principals in Georgia. While this was not a representative sample, it included large and small schools in rural and urban communities. The criticisms and suggestions of these principals and still more ideas by panel members formed the basis for new revisions of the questionnaire and finally the finished form.

The final General School Characteristics Questionnaire consisted of six parts. The first was devoted to school policies, practices, and plant. Questions included here were on the type of school, special classes, grading and advancement policies, physical condition of the school, and average class size. The next section concerned the number, training, and characteristics of the teaching staff. Then came questions about the students: enrollment, dropouts, percentage of graduates going on to college, remedial work, and the like. Next followed a section concerning characteristics of the community, such as PTA activity, type of area served by the school, tax rate, per-pupil expenditures, and community facilities. Another section asked about the age, experience, and training of the principal himself. At the end of the questionnaire we printed a long list of high school courses, grouped by broad subject matter areas. Here the principal indicated the courses offered in grades 9 to 12 in his school.

Virtually all of the questionnaire was in multiple choice form so that the principal could indicate his answer to a question by marking one (or, in some cases, several) responses. A few items were set up for write-in answers. These were confined to questions requiring a numerical response, such as number of days in the school year, per-pupil expenditure, and facts about enrollment.

3

The final questionnaire is too long to reproduce here, but the kind of information it provided can be illustrated by presenting some of the data supplied by three different schools. The three examples given below are not typical or representative, but were taken from the Project files for purposes of illustration. These examples show the type of descriptive picture which the questionnaire material provides. No conclusions should be drawn on the basis of the data presented here, since these descriptions do not include all of the information obtained about these three schools. They are presented only to illustrate the areas of coverage in the questionnaire.

School 1. This is a large, eastern, metropolitan public school with total enrollment for Grades 9, 10, 11, and 12 of 1795 boys

and 1880 girls. It is a fully accredited four-year high school operating on a school year of 192 days. Each day is composed of
seven 45-minute periods. Classes average 36 students who are
assigned 2–3 hours of homework a day. This school provides
several kinds of recognition for superior work, an advanced curriculum in all courses for superior students, and separate classes
for students with special talents. Separate classes are also available for the mentally retarded, for those with reading and speech
difficulties, and for rapid learners. Students earn numerical
grades (e.g., 75, 85, 95) based upon how well they have
mastered the subject matter. These grades are used as the principal basis for assigning students to instructional classes. Summer school and adult education courses are offered. Enrollment
is down somewhat from the preceding year; daily absenteeism
averages about 4%; and the administrative assistant who filled out
the questionnaire for review by the principal notes that the
school needs additional personnel in administrative, supervisory,
guidance, teaching, and clerical positions.

The school building is about 22 years old, but was renovated
less than three years ago. It is equipped with a library (more
than 2700 books), cafeteria, gym, athletic field, auditorium, various laboratories, and movie, radio, TV, phonograph, and public
address equipment. A wide variety of extra-curricular activities
and clubs are available.

All of the teachers are employed full-time, and about 55%
of them are men. Nearly all of the teachers have a master's degree; all are state-certified; they average more than 15 years
of full-time teaching experience. Beginning teachers start at
$4500–$4999 per year. Teacher turnover last year was about 4%.

Pupil transfers last year account for less than 4% of enrollment;
less than 9% of the boys and girls entering 10th grade drop out
before graduation; about three-fourths go on to college. Delinquency rate is about 1%. Less than 4% of the students take remedial math, remedial reading, or remedial English, and only
about 7% take repeat work in summer school.

More than 63% of the parents are members of the PTA, which
meets about once every five weeks to discuss school-parent relations problems. The area served by the school includes an equal
number of apartments and homes in a moderately expensive

urban residential area. No citizens' group has studied the school recently. Per-pupil expenditures last year were about $560. Many community facilities such as concerts, theater, library, museum, and scout activities are readily available.

The principal of this school is a man in his late 50's. He has had about 17 years' experience as a principal and has been head of this school for seven years. He holds a doctor's degree and has had more than 50 credits in education courses.

The courses offered in this school cover a wide range of commercial and college-preparatory subjects. A few vocational and shop courses are also offered.

School 2. This is a small, midwestern public school with total enrollment (for Grades 9–12) of 96 boys and 107 girls. It is a state-accredited 12-year school operating on a school year of 178 days composed of eight or more 45-minute periods each day. Classes average 24 to 29 students, who are assigned 1 to 2 hours of homework a day and have nine or more study halls per week. This school provides special-group, separate classes only for blind students. It has no accelerated curricula. It recognizes superior achievement only through a "dean's list" and the privilege of taking additional work. Numerical grades are assigned primarily on the basis of subject matter achievement and are used in combination with tests and staff judgment to make class assignments. There is no summer school. Only non-credit vocational courses are offered for adults. Enrollment is about the same as last year, with about 4% average daily absenteeism.

The school building is about seven years old and was painted and renovated less than three years ago. It has a library of about 1650 books; a cafeteria, gym, athletic field, auditorium, and science labs. The school is equipped to utilize motion pictures and radio for instructional purposes. Extra-curricular activities are not as broad and varied as in School 1, but include intramural athletics (boys and girls), band, school papers, dramatics, subject matter clubs, dances, and boys' inter-school athletics.

In contrast to School 1, there is no homogeneous grouping and no acceleration is permitted. The school employs ten full-time teachers, of whom seven are men. All of the teachers have a bachelor's degree; none have any higher degree; and only one or two have had any graduate training. All of the teachers are state-certified and average 15 years or more of full-time teaching experience. Beginning teachers start at $3500–$3999 per year. Turnover last year was zero.

Transfers last year were less than 4% of pupil enrollment, while dropouts from 10th grade on averaged about 15%. Only 15% of the boys and 5% of the girls go on to college. Delinquency rate was about 1%.

Only 10% of the parents are members of the PTA, which meets monthly, and no citizens' group has recently studied the school. The school serves a rural-farm area in which the residences are primarily moderate-priced homes about 25–29 years old. Per-pupil expenditure last year was about $233. Community facilities include a library, 4–H clubs, Scouts, and a public recreation center.

The principal of the school is a man in his early 50's who has spent all of his 17 years' teaching and administrative experience in this school. He holds a 4-year degree with 50 or more credits in education.

The courses offered are those of a comprehensive high school, but are considerably less varied than those of School 1. No fine arts are offered. Latin is the only language offered (compared with courses in Spanish, French, Latin, and Hebrew in School 1). Four agriculture courses are offered.

School 3.   This is a moderate sized, non-public school, located in the largest city in a western state. It has a total enrollment of 196 boys and 352 girls in the upper four of its 12 grades. It is fully accredited and operates on a 177-day school year, with six periods of 55 or more minutes per day. Classes average 28 students, who are given 2 to 3 hours per day of homework and no study halls. Special, separate classes are provided only for students with reading and math difficulty. A "dean's list," special awards, and accelerated math, science, and language curricula are provided for superior students. Numerical grades are assigned primarily on the basis of subject matter achievement and are used with tests and staff judgment to make class assignments. Students may attend summer school to take new courses or to repeat work. No adult education is offered. In contrast to Schools 1 and 2, religious education is contained in the regular curriculum. Enrollment is about the same as last year, with daily absenteeism averaging around 7%. Administrative, supervisory, guidance, and clerical personnel are reported to be needed.

The building is less than five years old and is equipped with a library of more than 2700 books. It has essentially the same equipment as Schools 1 and 2. Extra-curricular activities include school government, magazine, athletics, subject matter clubs, glee clubs and band, drama, debate, and religious clubs. Many courses are grouped homogeneously and there are several educational tracks, but no acceleration is permitted.

The school employs 23 full-time teachers and 10 regular part-time teachers; only 15% of the full-time teachers are men. Of the full-time teachers, 13 have the bachelor's degree while 10 have the master's degree. About 95% are state-certified. Only 55% are teaching in their major area of preparation. Starting salaries are from $3500–$3999 per year and average full-time teaching experience is 13 years.

Pupil transfers last year account for about 7% of enrollment. Delinquency and dropout rates are nil. However, only a quarter of the boys and 45% of girls go on to college. Less than 4% of the students take repeat or remedial summer work, but 7% are in remedial math and 12% in remedial reading or remedial English classes.

More than 63% of parents are members of the monthly PTA. No citizens' group has recently studied the school. Pupils attending the school come from areas scattered over the entire city and from all types of homes. Per-pupil expenditure last year (not comparable to public schools for various reasons) was reported as $100. Community resources include a library, a museum, concerts, and scout activities.

The principal of this school is a woman in her late 30's who has had about 17 years of teaching experience. She has been a principal less than five years and this is her first year as principal of this school. She holds a master's degree and has had about 45 credit hours of education courses.

Courses offered are those of a general comprehensive high school. Latin, French, and Spanish are given, but very little is offered in industrial arts and nothing in trade and vocational education. Several courses on religion are offered, as are music and fine arts.

4

In summary, the General School Characteristics Questionnaire was developed to be useful for future educational research. It was intended to deal with as many important areas as the school principal could reasonably be expected to take the time to cover.

It should be noted, however, that broad as the information requested in the questionnaire may be, it forms only a small part of those important questions which might have been asked. As suggested earlier, the difficult task which faced the staff and advisory panel was not what to include, but what to exclude. Decisions were made on the basis of which items of information seemed most important to the analysis of the other data being collected; which items seemed most important in their own right; and which items appeared to be reasonably accessible to the school principal.

Procedures and results of analyzing the information that has been gathered will be described in subsequent reports.

13 The Questionnaires: Surveying School Guidance Programs

This chapter takes up the two questionnaires designed to provide us with facts about school guidance programs. The guidance activities and the counselors who operate them are subjects of our consideration now.

We sketch the need for guidance in American schools and the purposes that counselors and guidance programs serve. This is followed by a statement of TALENT's purposes in gathering this information — to get facts about the current status of guidance in the nation; and to find out how guidance affects students. The development of the questionnaires is reviewed briefly.

With this chapter we conclude the description of our fact-gathering and fact-analysis activities of the first phase of Project TALENT.

Since the 1920's, educational objectives have specified the need for an expert to help the student and his parents decide on educational and vocational goals. However, the tests and methods needed for best determining these goals were only at the beginning of their development. Little emphasis, for example, was placed on the use of tests, partly because an adequate number of reliable and valid tests were not available. Even less emphasis was placed on helping students to understand themselves, because the techniques of personal counseling had not yet been developed.

The past forty years have seen guidance and counseling increasingly stressed in a well-organized school program. In years past, it was thought to be the sole duty and prerogative of parents, minister, priest, rabbi, or teacher to guide and counsel our youth. However, parents and others untrained in guidance do not always have the information needed in a rapidly changing world. There are many reasons for this. The number of boys and girls enrolled in public high schools has grown year by year and it is often difficult for many teachers, due to large classes, to know their students and their problems intimately. Year after year, too, the curriculum has expanded to provide for college preparatory, business, vocational, and agricultural courses. Many schools now offer courses for slow learners, fast learners, gifted children, and the physically and mentally handicapped. At the same time, the number and variety of occupations and careers have multiplied.

Though all of education is concerned with the progress of the individual child, guidance workers and counselors have begun to assume specialized roles in helping young people toward their life goals. These specialists are often trained more intensively than most classroom teachers to work with the child on problems which are not directly related to his academic program. The specialists may help him work out plans for a college education or other training after graduation. They may aid in obtaining information about scholarships or college loans. They may help him learn more about occupations in order that he might make a wise choice of careers.

In order to carry out their duties, guidance people should have, as part of their training and experience, study in the construction, administration, analysis, and interpretation of tests; in analysis and diagnosis of the individual; in counseling theory, techniques, and practices; and in professional standards. They should be acquainted with information on college requirements, occupations, and job opportunities.

The guidance program, then, may be expected to carry out a number of functions. Recently, the United States Office of Education[1] listed six functions:

"1. Analysis: Helping the student get the facts about himself — from test results, cumulative records, and other means of identifying potentialities and interests.

2. Information: Giving him the facts about his environment — about educational and occupational opportunities and requirements.

3. Orientation: Helping him get acquainted with the school program and educational and vocational opportunities and requirements.

4. Counseling: Helping him to develop self-understanding and to develop his educational and occupational plans.

5. Placement: Helping him carry out those plans.

6. Follow-up: Determining how his plans worked out and how effectively the educational program served him."

2

To get facts about the current status of guidance in the nation, we constructed two questionnaires that inquired about guidance efforts in the schools. We wanted information on the school's facilities for guidance, administrative arrangements for guidance, and the extent to which tests are used. We wanted to learn about the ways in which guidance fits into the over-all school program, by determining, for example, whether larger schools tend to make more adequate provisions for guidance than smaller schools. We also wanted information on the education, experience, and interests of counselors.

We wanted to find out how guidance programs affect the student's aspirations and plans for college. We wanted to see how guidance programs affect what students do, including dropping out of high school, attending college, obtaining a scholarship or a student loan, or choosing an appropriate vocation.

As we proceeded with the development of the questionnaire, we met several times with our advisers on the Guidance and Counseling Panel to get their ideas and suggestions on the make-up and nature of the questionnaire. The first questionnaire sub-

---

[1] Sievers, F. L., "For Better Understanding," *School Life.* 1959, I, 3.

mitted to the panel included, in a single form, questions about the guidance program and about the counselors. After reviewing this form, staff and panel agreed that the questions about the counselors should be presented in a separate form, so that each counselor in a school could answer questions about his own education and experiences. Subsequently, we developed two questionnaires, the first of which was to be answered by the guidance officer, giving the facts about the school's guidance program. The second questionnaire was designed for the individual counselor and asked questions about his education, qualifications, and experience in guidance. It was to be filled out by each staff member who spent 20 per cent or more of his time on guidance duties.

After these two forms had been developed, we tried them out by having them completed and commented upon by several counselors. A number of revisions were made on the basis of the comments of the counselors, and the revised forms were again submitted to our advisory panel for final review.

3

The final form of the Guidance Program Questionnaire included 24 pages of questions and more than 200 items of information. The Counselor's Questionnaire included six pages of questions and about 75 items of information.

The topics on which information was requested in each questionnaire were as follows:

The Guidance Program Questionnaire:

1. Scope of the guidance program. Does the school have a formal guidance program? If yes, how large is the guidance staff, how adequate are referral facilities in the community?
2. Types of aids and guidance provided. What kinds of problems are brought to counselors by students? When and how does the counselor schedule conferences with students and parents? Other questions asked about special courses related to guidance (such as occupations), and about the means used for imparting educational and vocational information.
3. Past growth. To what extent has the guidance program expanded in recent years?

4. Plans for expansion. What additions to the guidance program are expected in the next few years?
5. Testing. Does the school use nationally standardized tests and inventories — intelligence tests, aptitude batteries, interest inventories, and adjustment inventories? Are the tests administered to individuals or to entire classes? Are test results used to provide information to students and parents on school progress and on educational potential; to provide information to colleges and scholarship agencies; and to evaluate the school's progress in teaching subject matter?

The Counselor's Questionnaire:

1. Duties performed. What proportion of his time does the counselor devote to guidance duties as contrasted with other functions, such as teaching or administration? What proportion of the time devoted to guidance does he spend in the various guidance duties, such as testing, counseling, preparing reports?
2. Education and training. What courses and degrees related to guidance and counseling has the counselor pursued?
3. Experience. Counselors were asked to outline their experience in teaching and guidance.
4. Professional certification, participation, and interest. What professional organizations has the counselor joined? What meetings of professional societies does he attend? What professional magazines does he read? Has he obtained state certification?
5. Objectives. Each counselor was asked to indicate his concept of the contributions that a counselor should make to his students.
6. Theory and practice. This section asked the counselor to express his views on the activities that should ideally be included in a guidance program; and to describe how he would counsel a student. (A hypothetical problem of a student was presented briefly as a basis for reply.)

Analysis of the data from the two questionnaires will provide information on the number of schools that have formal guidance programs, as well as the number of full-time and part-time counselors. We will know the proportion of schools that have guidance programs, the proportion of counselors of each sex, the pro-

206   DESIGN FOR A STUDY OF AMERICAN YOUTH

portion of counselors with a master's degree, and the proportion of counselors in each region of the country.

Finally, we will have facts on which to build studies showing the ways in which guidance and counseling affect our students. We will conduct research to find out what role various guidance procedures play in helping students formulate college plans, obtain scholarships, and choose a vocation.

14 The Next Steps

In a real way, this book has been concerned with the past, present, and future in American education. The past has been characterized by subjective judgments as to the effectiveness of educational procedures — seldom have school practitioners had objective proof that the methods they were using were effective in achieving the goals claimed for them. The past has also been marked by uncertainty as to the importance of home, community, and personal factors in the development and utilization of human talents. Recall Commissioner of Education Derthick's statement in the Overview to this book as to the purposes of Project TALENT: ". . . to find out more about why some students learn and others do not, why some students do poorly in high school . . . while others who do well in high school fail to adjust to college. . . . to find out more about students' interests, career plans, and whether the courses they take are consistent with the life objectives they have set for themselves. . . . to determine why so much of the nation's human resources are lost and what schools, counselors, and parents can do to reduce this loss."

This book has traced some of the previous attempts to study these frustrating problems. We have noted that since the turn of the century our concepts of the nature of human talents have been slowly evolving. This development was speeded up by special military needs in World War II which resulted in large-scale studies of aptitudes and abilities.

The simple concept of general intelligence which provided the focus for Terman's series of studies entitled, "Genetic Studies of Genius," has been replaced by a relatively wide array of important and fairly distinct aptitudes. Many of these aptitudes have been shown to be closely related to job elements or practical intellectual activities. We, therefore, have had to expand the scope of our study from the hundreds studied by Terman to hundreds of thousands. Only with such a sample can we gain confidence in interpreting the significance of each of the thousands of patterns of aptitudes now identified.

As indicated in the middle chapters of the book, there has been a steady clarification of the significance of specific types of intellectual tasks. Means have been developed for getting efficient samples of the relative abilities of students to work effectively at these tasks. These relative abilities in the form of test scores are supplemented by self-descriptive statements in inventories which describe each individual's role, style, and preferences as he sees them. The third type of information about the individual describes his family background, his out-of-school activities, and his plans. All three of these types of information about each student must be considered together in interpreting the potential talents of a Robert, a Martha, or a Stephen.

To do this and to add to this picture descriptions of future experiences — both successes and failures — would be impossible without the high-speed electronic computers. With the aid of modern electronic scoring machines and document readers, all the information which each student recorded on answer sheets in March, 1960, was transferred to punched cards. Rosters containing reports of 37 scores for each student were returned to the schools by December, 1960.

With what data will these scores be compared as we proceed with the analysis? They will be compared with two main types, directed toward answering two broad series of questions. First, there will be the data regarding the educational and guidance programs of each school. These have already been obtained using the special school and guidance questionnaires described in the preceding chapters. These data will enable us to study questions about the relative importance of various factors in developing a student's talents. We hope to discover those things that a school can do which will contribute directly toward the full development of the student's potential. The second type of data will be obtained from the students at intervals of one, five, ten, and twenty years following their graduation from high school, when they will report about their activities and their careers. This should help us to answer many questions regarding the importance of specific patterns of talents for effective work in various fields.

Identifying and developing a student's talents is both important and desirable. But will he use his talents? Motivation, attitudes, and adjustment are becoming increasingly important. The role of the parent, the teacher, the counselor, and many others must also be studied if improvements are to be made.

We have attempted to document the historical background and the advances in technique and theory which, taken together, have led to the most coordinated single effort in this direction yet, Project TALENT. As a result of Project TALENT, the testing of thousands of students has been successfully completed. Information about their abilities, likes, dislikes, activities, plans, goals, homes, communities, and schools has been gathered. The information is at this moment undergoing analyses that will provide some of the answers to Commissioner Derthick's plea for information.

The next book in this series will report the results of analyzing the school and guidance information which has been collected. In it will be the most complete picture of the nation's schools ever assembled. It will be followed by a third book which will present the results of analyzing the student data. This book will describe the American high school student — his abilities and achievements — his characteristics and interests — his goals and background. Many of the interrelationships between school programs, community characteristics, and student information will be presented and discussed. Hypotheses about what causes these results will be presented.

Then, with the publication of Book No. 4, covering the first one-year follow-up, the long process of checking these hypotheses, revising them, and checking them again will begin. In the end, however, we hope to answer many basic questions about education, such as those proposed by the U.S. Commissioner of Education in the early chapters of this volume.

Much remains to be done. Many analyses have not yet been performed — indeed, many of the questions for which our data will provide answers have not yet been fully formulated. Nevertheless, Project TALENT is already taking steps toward the future. The first group of follow-up questionnaires has been mailed to students who were high school seniors when they were tested in 1960. These follow-up questionnaires will tell us what has happened to these students during the previous year. Have they gone to college? What have they studied? How well have they done? What are their career plans now? Their plans for military service? Have they taken a job? What kind? Do they like it? Do they plan to change or make it a career? These and many other items of information will be asked of every TALENT student one, five, ten, and twenty years after he has graduated from high school.

2

Consider Paul. When he took the TALENT tests, he was 17 years old and a senior. He lived in a one-family house in the suburbs of a large midwestern city. He had a newspaper route and enjoyed sports, building models, and building and repairing mechanical and electronic gadgets. He is the oldest of three boys of well-educated parents. His father is an engineer and his mother a part-time artist.

Paul said that he would like to go to college, but he expected to work a few years first. Costs were an important consideration to him, yet he would not be willing to borrow money to go to college. Paul's grades in high school were B's and C's, except for vocational courses where he had A's and B's. His test scores, however, showed a very high level of over-all ability, certainly ability to do college work. His scores for Information Test areas were, for the most part, better than those of 90 per cent of the 12th graders, and his total score for the Information Test exceeded that of 99 per cent of 12th graders. Similarly, he did very well on tests of Reading Comprehension, Creativity, Mechanical Reasoning, Abstract Reasoning, and Visualization. However, his English scores were low.

As a matter of fact, Paul was a great deal like Robert, whom we met in Chapter 1. Paul had college level ability, but low English scores and low high school grades would make it difficult for him to get into a first-rate college. Like Robert, Paul would like to go to college, but felt that it might not be possible for some time. While Paul was primarily interested in liberal arts rather than physical sciences, it seems, again like Robert, that test information and counseling might have helped him toward his goals.

Paul returned his first follow-up questionnaire in the spring of 1961. In it he said that he graduated from high school, but did not go to college. Instead he went to work as a full-time drafts-man. He already had changed his mind about his career, how-ever, and planned to enter college in the fall of 1961 in spite of the fact that he had doubled his starting salary in the job he held. He reported that his major reason for not going to college was that he was "tired" of school. Paul liked his job but planned to change to a related occupation involving more design work. He expects to be comfortably well off as a result of this job, and he feels that opportunity for promotion is the most important characteristic of a job.

As a contrast to Paul and Robert, let's consider Sam, a 17-year-old senior at a small town high school when he was tested. Sam is the fifth son of a skilled worker; his mother and father did not finish high school. Sam has been interested in sports, hunting, and fishing, and has had a newspaper route for several years. He expected to go to college by paying his own way and was willing to borrow money to do so. He was interested in chemistry and in research as a career. Unlike Robert and Paul, Sam devoted more time to his studies in high school and acquired a record of mostly A's and B's, with more A's than B's in science and mathematics.

Like Robert and Paul, Sam's test scores showed college apti-tude, though at a somewhat lower over-all level than either Rob-ert's or Paul's. His total Information Test score exceeded only 87 per cent of 12th graders, as compared with 95 per cent for Robert and 99 per cent for Paul. Sam obtained percentile ranks of 89, 85, and 62 respectively in Creativity, Mechanical Reason-ing, and Reading Comprehension. Visualization, Advanced Math, and English were at the 84th, 86th, and 68th percentiles, respectively.

What has happened to Sam since he graduated from high school? Sam, too, has returned his follow-up questionnaire and we find that he has enrolled at a state university where he is having a somewhat difficult time. He is earning C's, however, and expects to graduate and become an engineer. He has held no full-time job other than summer employment but plans to work summers to pay for college costs in the fall.

Robert, Paul, Sam. Three boys who are similar and yet dis-similar. How will these boys fare? Project TALENT will find out through its follow-up program. How much difference will

212 DESIGN FOR A STUDY OF AMERICAN YOUTH

their varied personal, community, and school backgrounds make in their success or failure in developing and using their abilities? Project TALENT will find out — not only for Paul, Robert, and Sam, but for the thousands of Pauls and Sams, Roberts and Jims, and Marys and Janes who will follow.

In later reports we shall describe the schools these students attended and also the interests, aptitudes, abilities, activities, and plans which the students have developed. It is hoped that these reports will lead to more effective plans for the identification, development, and use of all the talents of our young people.

Appendix

Appendix

SECTION A

Constructing the Experimental Test Battery

The table below, indicating the construction of over 2000 items, will give the readers some idea of the magnitude of the experimental battery. Two forms of each test (Form A and Form B) were prepared; half the students in the experimental tryout were tested with Form A and half with Form B. This made it possible to try out twice as many items.

As indicated in the last column of the table, some of the test names were changed in the final form, and because limitations on testing time available for the final battery made it necessary to shorten the battery somewhat, a few tests were eliminated altogether. The last column of this table then shows how the experimental battery ties in with the final battery.

Composition of Experimental Battery

TEST No.	TEST NAME	OP-TIONS PER ITEM	MINS. PER FORM	FORM A	FORM B	TOTAL	Test Name in Final Battery
1.	Vocabulary-Information Profile	5	170	355	354	696*	Information
2.	English: Active Vocabulary	5	8	15	15	30	****
3.	Effective Expression	2	9	10	10	20	***
4.	English Usage	2–5	14	24	24	48	***
5.	Sentence Structure	3	6	8	8	16	Punctuation. Section b. { Sentence Structure
6.	Punctuation	2–5	12	23	23	46	a. { Punctuation Marks
7.	Capitalization	2	15	71	71	71**	***
8.	Spelling	5	14	18	18	36	***
9.	Reading Comprehension	5	26	51	51	102	****
10.	Following Directions	5	12	15	15	30	***
11.	Disguised Words	5	3	25	25	50	
12.	Words in Sentences	5	12	20	20	40	Word Functions in Sentences
13.	Paired Associates	5	3	12	12	24	Memory for Words
14.	Sentence Completion	5	5	8	8	16	Memory for Sentences

No.	Experimental battery test						Final battery test
15.	Arithmetic Computation	5	20	60	60	60**	Mathematics I. Arithmetic Reasoning ***
16.	Arithmetic Reasoning	5	28	18	18	36	II. Introductory ****
17.	Mathematics A. (through Grade 9)	5 }	40	19	19	38	III. Advanced ***
18.	B. (Grades 10–12)	5 }		16	16	32	
19.	Verbal Reasoning	3	14	25	25	50	
20.	Abstract Reasoning	5	14	18	18	36	
21.	Mechanical Reasoning	2–5	12	24	24	48	
22.	Spatial A. Folding	5	8	18	18	36	Visualization in Two Dimensions
23.	Spatial B. Rotation-Reflection	5	4	16	16	32	Visualization in Three Dimensions ****
24.	Scale Reading	5	6	24	24	48	
25.	Name Comparison	2	6	100	100	100**	Clerical Checking ***
26.	Table Reading	5	3	70	70	70**	
27.	Form Perception	5	3	36	36	72	Object Inspection ***
28.	Creativity	5	16	15	15	30	
29.	Social Judgment	2	2	90	90	90**	Preferences
	TOTAL		1204	1203	1203	2003	

* 13 items (screening scale) are the same in both forms
** Same items in both forms
*** Same test name in final battery as experimental battery
**** Not in final battery

SECTION B

UNIQUENESS ANALYSIS

In determining whether a test in the experimental battery should be retained in the final battery, a crucial question is: "Does the test make any unique contribution to the battery?"

The answer to this question is affirmative — and the test is therefore acceptable — if the multiple correlation of the test with an optimally weighted composite of all the rest of the tests is significantly less than the maximum correlation consistent with the reliability of the variables correlated. This principle was formalized, and a procedure based on it was developed, by the senior author of this book.[1] This procedure consists in determining "uniqueness coefficients" for each variable, using the following formula:

$$U_i{}^2 = r_{ii} - \frac{R^2}{r_{cc}}$$

where $U_i{}^2$ = uniqueness coefficient for variable i

r_{ii} = reliability coefficient for variable i

R^2 = multiple correlation of variable i with the rest of the variables in the set

r_{cc} = reliability of the weighted composite of the independent variables

It is readily apparent that the uniqueness coefficient, U^2, represents the proportion of the test's variance corresponding to a component which is both reliable and completely free of overlap with any of the other tests.

[1] Flanagan, J. C., *Flanagan Aptitude Classification Tests: Technical Report.* Science Research Associates, Chicago, 1959.

A slightly modified version of this uniqueness analysis procedure was carried out on the experimental forms of the TALENT tests, on the basis of the tryout data. Fifty-two variables were involved, for each of which a multiple correlation with the 51 other variables was determined. An approximation of the uniqueness coefficient was determined by using a modification of the formula above. This formula is:

$$U'^2_i = r_{ii} - {}_sR^2$$

where U'^2_i = approximation of uniqueness coefficient

${}_sR^2 = R^2$ corrected by Wherry shrinkage formula[2]

The Wherry shrinkage formula is:

$${}_sR^2 = 1 - \frac{N-1}{N-n-1}(1-R^2)$$

where N = number of cases

n = number of independent variables

It will be noted that the chief way in which the formulas for U^2_i and U'^2_i differ is that in the latter the r_{cc} term is omitted. This expedient was necessary in the case of the TALENT analysis because it was not feasible to determine r_{cc} at the time. However, it is believed that this made relatively little difference since omission of the r_{cc} was the same as assuming it to equal unity — an assumption which is likely not to be too far from the truth when the composite (c) is based on so many test variables (51) and so many items (over 1000).

The 52 variables in the TALENT uniqueness analysis were 24 scales from the *Information Test* (then called the *Vocabulary-Information Profile Test*) and the other 28 variables shown in the table in Section A of the Appendix.

The uniqueness coefficients are shown in the table below, along with the reliability coefficients and $\bar{p}$ values. The latter are the averages of the item difficulty indices for the test. These

[2] Wherry, R. J., "A New Formula for Predicting the Shrinkage of the Coefficient of Multiple Correlation." *Annals of Mathematical Statistics*, 2: 440–457 (1939).

Table: Uniqueness Coefficients, Reliability Coefficients, and Other Data from Spring 1959 Tryout of Experimental Forms (Forms A and B)

Scale No.	Scale	No. of items A	No. of items B	No. of keyed items A	No. of keyed items B	r_{11}^{**} Grades 9–10 A	r_{11}^{**} Grades 9–10 B	r_{11}^{**} Grades 11–12 A	r_{11}^{**} Grades 11–12 B	U'^2 Grades 9–10 A	U'^2 Grades 9–10 B	U'^2 Grades 11–12 A	U'^2 Grades 11–12 B	$\bar{p}^{***}$ Grades 9–10 A	$\bar{p}^{***}$ Grades 9–10 B	$\bar{p}^{***}$ Grades 11–12 A	$\bar{p}^{***}$ Grades 11–12 B
1–01	Screening	13	13	13	13	.79	.43	.63	.56	.24	.21	.27	.38	.93	.85	.95	.94
1–02	Scientific Att.	7	7	7	7	.50	.49	.34	.42	.04	.09	−.02	.03	.57	.49	.64	.54
1–03	Vocabulary	10	10	10	10	.53	.54	.48	.50	−.00	.02	.00	.04	.53	.60	.58	.64
1–04	Literature	30	30	30	30	.80	.73	.79	.78	.13	.09	.09	.07	.37	.41	.45	.48
1–05	Music	15	15	15	15	.62	.60	.64	.60	.08	.14	−.03	.08	.35	.36	.41	.41
1–06	Art	10	10	10	10	.56	.45	.49	.54	.01	.05	−.01	.07	.51	.27	.55	.31
1–07	Social Studies	38	38	38	37	.82	.76	.82	.80	.09	.12	.11	.14	.36	.36	.43	.42
1–08	Mathematics	18	18	18	18	.80	.62	.85	.79	.10	.10	.13	.11	.36	.27	.45	.33
1–09	Physical Science	20	21	20	21	.72	.77	.76	.80	.05	.11	.06	.10	.39	.41	.45	.47
1–10	Bio. Sci. Nat. St.	15	14	15	14	.72	.45	.68	.52	.12	.01	.13	.06	.50	.32	.55	.33
1–11	Law	7	7	11	7	.38	.38	.41	.42	−.03	−.02	.02	.02	.34	.40	.41	.46
1–12	Medicine	11	11	11	11	.54	.57	.44	.50	.03	.03	.06	.03	.51	.56	.55	.62
1–13	Engin., Arch.	8	8	8	8	.39	.31	.40	.28	−.06	.07	.00	−.00	.50	.24	.56	.29
1–14	Aeronaut., Sp.	9	9	9	9	.45	.60	.54	.65	.04	.14	.05	.11	.26	.24	.30	.26
1–15	Electricity	17	17	17	17	.69	.69	.72	.74	.13	.14	.13	.11	.25	.35	.29	.40
1–16	Tools, Constr.	7	7	7	6	.52	.55	.50	.47	−.01	.12	−.03	.04	.45	.40	.49	.48
1–17	Motors, Mech.	6	6	6	6	.61	.32	.59	.40	.12	.05	.07	.04	.39	.38	.46	.46
1–18	Military	6	7	6	7	.50	.31	.51	.32	.11	.04	.10	.09	.27	.29	.32	.32
1–19	Acct., Bus., Sales	7	7	7	7	.29	.28	.34	.45	−.06	−.02	.00	.10	.50	.31	.56	.39
1–20	Farm, Ranch.	9	9	9	9	.44	.47	.44	.54	.06	.11	.12	.15	.45	.51	.49	.56
1–21	Bible	11	11	11	11	.46	.66	.46	.69	.09	.35	.14	.35	.39	.33	.42	.37
1–22	Home Economics	20	19	20	19	.55	.51	.52	.57	.17	.22	.15	.22	.36	.32	.41	.37
1–23	Outdoor Activ.	10	10	9	10	.38	.31	.35	.43	−.03	−.02	.03	.06	.39	.42	.43	.46
1–24	Sports	7	6	7	6	.33	.41	.38	.47	−.04	.12	.10	.17	.29	.34	.33	.37
	Other	44	44	44													
1–00	Total	355	354	355	352	.96	.94	.94	.96					.40	.38	.46	.44

Vocabulary-Information Profile Test — *Vocabulary Test*

220

					L	K	J	I	H	G	F	E	D	C	B	A
2-00	Eng: Active Vocab.	15	15	15	15	.70	.54	.65	.57	.12	.12	.14	.10	.54	.36	.61	.44
3-00	Eff. Expression	10	10	10	9	.55*	.38*	.47*	.34*	.17	.27	.16	.18	.69	.49	.78	.55
4-00	Eng. Usage	24	23	24	24	.62	.45	.46	.34	.09	.09	.02	.09	.58	.66	.64	.70
5-00	Sent. Structure	8	8	8	8	.72*	.66*	.73*	.61*	.27	.35	.37	.30	.63	.73	.71	.80
6-00	Punctuation	23	18	23	18	.58	.56	.46	.54	.11	.11	.06	.16	.32	.32	.38	.41
7-00	Capitalization	71	71	71	70	.89*	.90*	.81*	.82*	.61	.56	.46	.48	.85	.83	.89	.86
8-00	Spelling	18	18	18	18	.69	.53	.62	.58	.16	.17	.14	.23	.46	.42	.52	.46
9-00	Rd. Comp.	51	50	51	51	.85	.78	.84	.79	.08	.10	.11	.07	.57	.57	.64	.63
10-00	Follow. Directions	15	15	15	13	.73	.65	.68	.68	.12	.12	.15	.17	.58	.47	.66	.53
11-00	Lang: Disguis. Wd.	25	25	25	25	.81	.72	.80	.74	.30	.27	.33	.27	.40	.34	.46	.39
12-00	Wds. in Sen.	20	20	20	20	.76	.64	.77	.72	.26	.19	.28	.20	.27	.22	.33	.27
13-00	Pair. Assoc.	12	12	12	11	.81*	.78*	.78*	.81*	.51	.54	.54	.57	.60	.53	.66	.60
14-00	Sentence Completion	8	8	8	8	.66*	.66*	.64*	.59*	.40	.43	.45	.43	.62	.58	.66	.60
15-00	Arith. Computation	60	59	60	60	.89	.84	.83	.81	.22	.45	.31	.39	.78	.78	.84	.82
16-00	Arith. Reasoning	18	17	18	15	.78	.65	.78	.73	.15	.11	.14	.15	.47	.38	.56	.50
17-00	Math. A (through 9)	19	19	19	19	.64	.62	.74	.72	.10	.13	.16	.08	.22	.32	.27	.37
18-00	Math. B (10-12)	16	16	16	14	.46	.19	.58	.51	.16	.07	.10	.11	.09	.07	.14	.11
19-00	Verbal Reasoning	25	25	25	25	.68	.32	.67	.50	.17	.13	.15	.18	.42	.33	.50	.38
20-00	Abstr. Reasoning	18	18	18	17	.80	.65	.75	.65	.19	.21	.18	.20	.55	.56	.62	.61
21-00	Mech. Reasoning	24	24	24	24	.71	.69	.73	.74	.12	.17	.12	.17	.45	.47	.50	.52
22-00	Spatial A (Fold.)	18	17	18	18	.66	.67	.68	.63	.24	.30	.24	.25	.26	.29	.30	.33
23-00	Spatial B (Rot. Ref.)	16	16	16	16	.84	.83	.84	.85	.51	.51	.47	.49	.45	.56	.51	.61
24-00	Scale Reading	24	20	24	22	.76	.69	.74	.71	.19	.25	.16	.22	.50	.52	.56	.60
25-00	Name Comparison	100	100	100	100	—	.81	—	.68	—	.31	—	.28	.50	.55	.59	.56
26-00	Table Reading	70	70	70	70	.78	.74	.67	.66	.30	.32	.30	.28	.36	.36	.40	.42
27-00	Form Perception	36	35	36	33	.70	.59	.69	.61	.27	.28	.33	.31	.40	.42	.43	.44
28-00	Creativity	15	15	15	15	.61	.34	.60	.42	.17	.10	.14	.14	.33	.18	.39	.21
29-00	Social Judgments	90	90	90	90	.68	.71	.60	.60	.43	.46	.36	.38	.37	.38	.34	.35

* Split-half reliabilities on these tests; separately timed halves on others.

** For tests which have the same items in Forms A and B, the Part I and Part II items are reversed if the test has separately timed halves. (See table in Appendix Section A; ** footnote.)

All reliability coefficients in this table have been corrected by the Spearman-Brown formula.

*** $\bar{p} = \dfrac{M}{n}$ where M = mean score

n = number of keyed items

item difficulty indices range from .00 (extremely hard item) to 1.00 (extremely easy item).

The numbers of students on which the data in this table are based are as follows:

Grades	Test Form	N
9–10	A	1602
	B	1026
11–12	A	952
	B	945

SECTION C

Composition of the Final Battery

The table below shows the tests in logical (*not* chronological) arrangement. In this respect it differs from Table 4 (in Chapter 10), in which the chronological order in which the tests were administered is shown. A comparison of the table below with Table 4 will show how the various parts of the battery were made to mesh together into a unified testing schedule which would make full use of the available time and at the same time would provide the student with sufficient change of content and of pace to prevent boredom and encourage maximum effort.

APTITUDE AND ACHIEVEMENT TESTS

	1 Options per Item	2 No. of Items	3 No. of Minutes Working Time*	4 No. of Scores	5 Scoring Formula**
Information Test					
Part I	5	(252)	90	(16)	
Subscales				(15)	
1. Screening		12		1	R
2. Vocabulary		21		1	R
3. Literature		24		1	R
4. Music		13		1	R
5. Social Studies		24		1	R
6. Mathematics		23		1	R
7. Physical Science		18		1	R
8. Biological Science		11		1	R
9. Scientific Attitude		10		1	R
10. Aeronautics and Space		10		1	R
11. Electricity and Electronics		20		1	R
12. Mechanics		19		1	R
Tools and Construction		(10)			
Motors and Mechanisms		(9)			
13. Farming		12		1	R
14. Home Economics		21		1	R
Cooking		(11)			
Other		(10)			
15. Sports		14		1	R
Total		(252)		1	R
Part II	5	143	35		
Subscales		***		***	$R - \dfrac{W}{4}$
Parts I + II combined		(395)	(125)		
Vocabulary Scale		(30)		1	
Grand Total		(395)		1	

223

	1 Options per Item	2 No. of Items	3 No. of Minutes Working Time*	4 No. of Scores	5 Scoring Formula*
Memory for Sentences					
Study	–	(40 sentences)	6	–	
Test	5	16	10	1	R
Memory for Words					
Study		(24 words)	2	–	
Practice		(24)	2	–	
Test	5	24	4	1	R
Disguised Words					
Directions	–	–	1		
Test	5	30	3	1	R
English			52		
1. Spelling	5	16		1	R
2. Capitalization	2	33		1	R
3. Punctuation					
a. Punctuation Marks	3–5	(16)		–	
b. Sentence Structure	3	(11)		–	
Punctuation Total		27		1	R
4. English Usage	3–5	25		1	R
5. Effective Expression	3–5	12		1	R
Total		(113)		1	R
Word Functions in Sentences					
Directions	–	–	2½		
Test	5	24	15	1	R
Reading Comprehension	5	48	30	1	R
Creativity	5	20	20	1	R
Mechanical Reasoning	3–5	20	11	1	R
Visualization in Two Dimensions	5	24	4	1	R
Visualization in Three Dimensions	5	16	9	1	R
Abstract Reasoning	5	15	11	1	R
Mathematics			50	(5)	
Part I. Arithmetic Reasoning	5	16		1	R
Part II. Introductory	5	24		1	R
Subtotal (Parts I + II)	5	40		1	R
Part III. Advanced	5	14		1	R
Total (Parts I + II + III)	5	54		1	R
Arithmetic Computation	5	72	9	1	R–3W
Table Reading	5	72	3	1	R–W
Clerical Checking	2	74	3	1	R–3W
Object Inspection	5	40	33	1	R–W
Miscellaneous					
Preferences Test	2	166	3	1	–
Themes	–	2	10+		–

NVENTORIES

	1 Options per Item	2 No. of Items	3 No. of Minutes Working Time*	4 No. of Scores
tudent Activities Inventory	5	(150)	20	
Regular Scales				10
Sociability		12		
Social Sensitivity		9		
Impulsiveness		9		
Vigor		7		
Calmness		9		
Tidiness		11		
Culture		10		
Leadership		5		
Self-Confidence		12		
Mature Personality		24		
Experimental Scales				3
Conventionality		4		
Theoreticality		8		
Group-Centeredness		6		
Miscellaneous		24		–
nterest Inventory	5	205	20	(16)
Part I. Occupations		(122)		
Part II. Activities		(83)		
Scales				
1. Science		24		1
2. Computation		10		1
3. Mechanical-Technical		15		1
4. Skilled Trades		18		1
5. Literary-Linguistic		15		1
6. Social Service		11		1
7. Public Service		11		1
8. Musical		5		1
9. Artistic		6		1
10. Business Management		14		1
11. Sales		6		1
12. Office Work		9		1
13. Labor		10		1
14. Farming		7		1
15. Outdoor Recreation		3		1
16. Sports		8		1
Miscellaneous		33		
tudent Information Blank	2–36	394	80	

* Does not include the time used for giving directions except where otherwise ndicated. (The exceptions occur where comprehension of directions is considered n integral part of the testing time allowance.)

** R = no. of right responses; W = no. of wrong responses.

*** The scoring of Part II is extremely flexible, since each student's responses to he individual items were punched on cards. In scoring Part II, it is planned to ombine the items in many ways.

SECTION D

The Original Student Activities Inventory Traits

The procedures used to develop the Student Activities Inventory resulted in a group of 18 narrow traits. Further work on these 18 traits enabled the staff to describe them more fully and to make some suggestions as to their implications and importance. While some of the traits were later combined and others dropped, the material below provides an idea of what each of the original traits was like. For each trait the name is given, then a description, a sample of the kind of activity concerned, and finally some comments.

1. Leadership. This trait concerns activities such as taking charge, giving orders and actively seeking responsibilities. It is commonly identified as part of the dominance factor.

Sample:
I like to make decisions.

The tendency to seek responsibility and to seek to "take charge" is considered desirable by many people, and is a major factor in vocational and educational choices.

2. Vigor. This trait concerns the activity level of a person, primarily on the physical side. It is related to the somewhat broader factor of general drive, which would include high levels of both physical and mental activity. It is fairly stable and easily observable in the high school student.

Sample:
I play games for hours without getting tired.

Measurement of this factor will make it possible to study the extent to which persons with certain abilities and interests are successful in proportion to their drive level. It will aid in defining creativity with respect to the amount of pure activity involved. It will make possible the correlation of vigor with other aspects of ability such as productivity, scholastic aptitude, achievement in various subject matter areas, overall adjustment, and ingenuity.

3. *Productivity.* This trait concerns the ability to get things done, particularly in good time. The emphasis is on quantity. No assumptions are made as to the quality of the products other than that they are acceptable, *i.e.*, meet the required minimum standards. Essential characteristics of this trait seem to include clear understanding of task goals; strong need for achievement oriented toward accomplishments and completed products; interests stable enough to allow the completion of products; and habitually good concentration and efficient utilization of time and effort. This trait is closely related to persistence, vigor, and responsibility.

Sample:
I work fast and get a lot done.

In measuring the extent to which a person tends to produce efficiently in good time, we are getting a measure of one of the aspects of human ability that society values most. This measure forms a good criterion against which to relate other kinds of personality, training, and background variables. Especially interesting are relationships with biographical information and with school educational practices.

4. *Tidiness.* This involves a tendency to want to keep things neat and orderly. It is probably related to a more general factor of compulsiveness, but as a trait it can be clearly defined and easily observed at the high school level.

Sample:
I do my homework as neatly as possible.

Tidiness is probably of lesser consequence to the study *per se*. However, to the extent that tidiness relates to rigidity or lack of adaptability on the one hand, or to executive, administrative, or organizing ability on the other, it can be of considerable importance to educational and vocational planning and success.

5. *Sociability.* This refers to a tendency to like and need to be with people, *i.e.*, gregariousness. This is a highly important and observable aspect of behavior at the high school level.

Sample:
I take a big part in social activities.

The importance of sociability to many of the factors being studied in the project is obvious. Few, if any, people really work alone, and the extent to which people have and make use of the ability to relate to others is a prominent determining factor in the direction and success of their later vocational and educational efforts. Certainly one of the objectives of guidance and counseling has often been to assist the student in getting along with people in more adequate fashion.

6. *Self-confidence.* This includes a basic personal security manifested in confidence in one's own worth and social acceptability. It implies willingness to proceed on one's own and a certain independence of thought and action. It is related to self-sufficiency, and it correlates moderately well with maturity as well. It appears important and rateable at the high school level.

Sample:
I'm equal to any occasion.

By and large, self-confidence is a highly desired trait. Again, measures of self-confidence can be related to many of the objectives of the study: biographical information, creativity, productivity, ingenuity, achievement, effects of guidance and counseling, and the prediction of vocational and educational success.

7. *Cheerfulness.* This trait concerns the tendency to "make the best of things," to be lighthearted, to look on the bright side, and to avoid a pessimistic view. It is commonly mentioned in the literature as a well-defined, fairly stable trait. It is one that is easily observed at the high school level, and is probably of considerable importance to future behavior.

Sample:
I am good-natured most of the time.

This trait, a generally desirable one, probably has an important bearing on the choices, plans and decisions made by high school students. It is likely that such choices are highly influenced by one's general outlook on life — that is, optimism, hopefulness, eagerness, and cheerfulness, versus pessimism, sadness, and seriousness. It is possible that measurement of this trait will prove to discriminate between various kinds of occupational choices, such as service occupations as opposed to research occupations.

8. *Culture.* This trait concerns a tendency to appreciate aesthetic things and to display refinement, culture, and good taste. Historically these items have been closely related to the often-discussed masculinity-femininity factor. Culture is probably a little less observable in the high school setting than many of the other traits, but it bears important implications for future behavior.

Sample:
I enjoy works of art.

Although this particular trait appears to have somewhat less implication for the study as a whole, it has some bearing on the selection of hobbies, avocations, and vocational choices.

9. *Talkativeness.* This is a clearly recognizable aspect of behavior of considerable import. It is characterized by a desire to talk about anything and everything with almost anybody, sometimes to the eventual discomfiture of the talker. Talkativeness seems to be related to vigor, to sociability, and perhaps to lack of self-discipline. Even so it seems to have some essence of its own. Bright children are often talkative, as might be expected from their superior verbal facility. Yet average to dull children may also display this trait.

Sample:
I start conversations easily with strangers.

The measurement of talkativeness relates somewhat less well to the objectives of the overall study than do other traits. Certainly, however, the relationship of talkativeness to such factors as vigor, sociability, self-confidence, etc. would be of considerable interest, if somewhat outside the stated measurement goals of the study. Talkativeness might also be interestingly, perhaps negatively, related to productivity, ingenuity, and vocational success.

10. Impulsiveness. This trait concerns the tendency to make snap decisions, to act without full consideration, to do and say things on impulse and whim. It is probably related to lack of self-discipline, and perhaps indirectly to drive. This appears to be a trait which is observable, but perhaps somewhat difficult to self-rate.

Sample:
I usually act on the first plan that comes to mind.

The measurement of impulsiveness bears an important relationship to stability of occupational and educational choice, the number of switches in program and occupation, effectiveness of counseling, and factors involved in making decisions and plans.

11. Persistence. This trait refers to a tendency to keep working on something until it is finished or accomplished. It is undoubtedly related to drive and also to self-discipline, since persistence really involves drive which is directed toward some goal. This is observable at the high school level and is very important to future behavior.

Sample:
I usually stick to the things I start until I finish them.

Since this trait refers to a tendency to persevere in working toward some long-range goal, it is of importance to relate it to any of the long-term aspects of the data being gathered. It is especially important in evaluating satisfaction with educational and career choices, and in comparing current choices with follow-up activities.

12. Calmness. This concerns the ability to react appropriately to emotional situations rather than displaying extremes of elation, temperament, excitability, depression, etc. Evenness and smoothness of temperament are the observable characteristics, and the trait is considered highly important. This trait is clearly related to the one described as mature personality.

Sample:
I rarely lose my temper.

Many of the objectives of the study have to do with the extent to which the student achieves a satisfactory adjustment to his environment and its demands. Therefore this measure is highly related and highly important to the child's ability to integrate himself into his school and work situation in such a way that he can take advantage of his abilities and prior achievements. Measuring calmness will make it possible to study the extent to which emotional stability is related to occupational-vocational success, effectiveness of counseling, efficient decision-making, etc.

13. Social Adjustment. This trait concerns reactions and interactions with others. At one end, it concerns helpfulness and cooperation; at the other, behavior which is distinctly and overtly anti-social and/or hostile. This trait is extremely important in the high school setting. It is probably related to sociability, but it has often been identified as a separate factor.

Sample:
People seem to think I'm cooperative.

Measurement along this dimension is very important in attempting to determine what conditions of background, interest, and aptitude go along with the desire to help and cooperate and to work efficiently with others.

14. Theoreticality. This concerns the tendency to be a thinker rather than a doer; to prefer intellectual activity of all kinds to working with tangible things. It has been identified as a distinct factor in some studies, but is probably related to sociability and self-sufficiency. It is important to one's general behavior and is probably easily observed and rated. It is very likely to be a stable characteristic at the high school level.

Sample:
I spend a lot of time by myself thinking.

This dimension is extremely important with respect to the kind of vocation selected and the extent to which the person is concerned with ideas, concepts, and philosophies, as opposed to society, people, and things. Theoreticality should bear a relationship to effectiveness of counseling, educational and vocational choices, and decision-making.

15. Responsibility. This trait involves not the active seeking of responsibility but the willingness to accept and discharge responsibilities, even though they be distasteful, to the best of one's ability. The person who scores high on this trait has a strong sense of duty and can be depended upon to carry out his assignment even at personal discomfort. Responsibility is observable in high school. It is related to the traits of mature personality, conformity, and persistence.

Sample:
People say they can count on me.

Responsibility, or the willingness to accept and discharge responsibilities, is certainly one of the most important of the work attitudes or traits, and as such it is related to almost all of the variables under study.

16. Social Sensitivity. This trait involves the ability to put oneself in another's place. The person with social sensitivity is aware of and concerned about the feelings and desires of others.

Sample:
I don't like to see someone's feelings hurt.

The trait is perhaps somewhat rare in high school; nevertheless it constitutes an important part of behavior. It is related somewhat to the traits of sociability and mature personality.

17. Group-centeredness. This trait involves concern for the good or welfare of the group as opposed to self-centeredness. It is amenable to self-rating, and it is undoubtedly important to future behavior. However it may be less observable, behaviorally, at the high school level than some other traits. Group-centeredness tends to be related to sociability, mature personality, and conformity.

Sample:
I'd give up my place on the team, if it meant the team would win.

The trait of placing the advancement of the group ahead of one's own is highly important to getting along in today's complex, highly-peopled society. Measurements here might be related to many background factors, to many other personality variables — such as leadership and vigor — and to various family and cultural factors, as well as to vocational and educational success.

18. Conventionalism. This concerns the trait of conforming and adapting to rules and conventions, whether one likes them or not. It involves high respect for the rule-making body (not necessarily society, but perhaps a sub-culture) with which an identification is achieved. It is related to group-orientation and sociability, and bears a negative relationship to self-sufficiency.

Sample:
I obey rules whether I like them or not.

Perhaps the most interesting relationship would be that between conventionalism and the creativity test. Productivity and originality are some of the other areas where relationships with conventionalism should be of value for study. The effect of conventionalism on decision-making, including its promptness and its adequacy, and on predictability of occupation and occupational success are also certainly of interest.

SECTION E

TYPES OF SCORES OBTAINED FROM
ANSWER SHEETS A AND C

It has been noted that 60 scores were obtained for each student in the initial scoring, but that only 37 of them were included in the reports to the schools. The remaining 23 scores were not reported since all of them were either for tests of an experimental character or they were of such a nature that they would have little direct utility for the schools. However, all 60 of the scores are slated for future analysis since further study of them — including the 23 not reported to the schools — should provide much useful and important knowledge.

In addition to the 60 scores obtained for all students, 53 additional scores were obtained for the previously mentioned 4 per cent sample, primarily for research purposes. In most cases this involved the computation of an additional type of score (for instance, a number-of-items-attempted score) on subtests for which one type of score (for instance, a number-right score) had already been derived for all students. For a few subtests, however, the only scores obtained were those for the 4% sample.

The following table shows the 60 scores obtained for all students, including the 37 scores reported to the schools, and the 53 additional scores obtained for the 4% sample.

These symbols are used in the table to represent the different kinds of scores:

$$R = \text{number right}$$
$$R{-}W = \text{no. right minus no. wrong}$$
$$R{-}3W = \text{no. right minus 3 times no. wrong}$$
$$A = \text{no. of items attempted}$$

When any of the above symbols appears in **bold print** it indicates that the score was reported to the schools.

Code No.	Test	Scores Obtained For All Students	Scores Obtained For 4% Sample
Information Test — Part I			
101.	Screening	R	A
102.	Vocabulary	R	A
103.	Literature	R	A
104.	Music	R	A
105.	Social Studies	R	A
106.	Mathematics	R	A
107.	Physical Sciences	R	A
108.	Biological Sciences	R	A
109.	Scientific Attitude	R	A
110.	Aeronautics and Space	R	A
111.	Electricity and Electronics	R	A
112.	Mechanics	R	A
112–A.	Tools, Construction	–	R,A
112–B.	Motors and Mechanisms	–	R,A
113.	Farming	R	A
113–A.	Farm	–	R,A
113–B.	Ranch	–	R,A
114.	Home Economics	R	A
114–A.	Cooking	–	R,A
114–B.	Other	–	R,A
115.	Sports	R	A
190.	Total	R	–
Other Tests			
211.	Memory for Sentences	R	A
212.	Memory for Words	R	A
220.	Disguised Words	R	A
	English		
231.	Spelling	R	A
232.	Capitalization	R	A
233.	Punctuation	R	A
233–A.	Sec. *a.* Punctuation Marks	–	–
233–B.	Sec. *b.* Sentence Structure	–	R,A
234.	English Usage	R	A
235.	Effective Expression	R	A
230.	English Total	R	A
240.	Word Functions in Sentences	R	A
250.	Reading Comprehension	R	A
260.	Creativity	R	A
270.	Mechanical Reasoning	R	A
281.	Visualization in 2 Dimensions	R	A
282.	Visualization in 3 Dimensions	R	A
290.	Abstract Reasoning	R	A
	Mathematics		
311.	I. Arithmetic Reasoning	R	A
312.	II. Introductory	R	A
320.	Subtotal (I + II)	R	A
333.	III. Advanced	R	A
340.	Total (I + II + III)	R	A

Code No.	Test	Scores Obtained For All Students	Scores Obtained For 4% Sample
410.	Arithmetic Computation	R,R–3W,A	–
420.	Table Reading	R,R–W,A	–
430.	Clerical Checking	R,R–3W,A	–
440.	Object Inspection	R,R–W,A	–
500.	Preferences	A	–
Student	*Activities Inventory*		
601.	Sociability	R	–
602.	Social Sensitivity	R	–
603.	Impulsiveness	R	–
604.	Vigor	R	–
605.	Calmness	R	–
606.	Tidiness	R	–
607.	Culture	R	–
608.	Leadership	R	–
609.	Self-confidence	R	–
610.	Mature Personality	R	–
611.	Conventionality	–	R
612.	Theoreticality	–	R
613.	Group-Centeredness	–	R

INDEX